# Yankee Doodle Dandy

# Yankee Doodle Dandy

## The Life and Times of Tod Sloan

JOHN DIZIKES

Yale University Press    New Haven and London

Published with assistance from the Louis Stern Memorial Fund.

Printed in the United States of America.

Library of Congress Cataloging-in-Publication Data
Dizikes, John, 1932–   .
Yankee Doodle Dandy : the life and times of Tod Sloan /
John Dizikes.
p.   cm.
Includes bibliographical references and index.
ISBN 0-300-08334-3 (alk. paper)
1. Sloan, Tod, 1874–1933.   2. Jockeys—United States—
Biography.   3. Jockeys—England—Biography.   I. Title.

SF336.S553 D58   2000
798.4'0092 B 21     00-033403

A catalogue record for this book is available from
the British Library.

The paper in this book meets the guidelines for
permanence and durability of the Committee on Production
Guidelines for Book Longevity of the Council
on Library Resources.

10 9 8 7 6 5 4 3 2 1

*In memory of Eloise and Page Smith*

A person does not (as I had imagined) stand motionless and clear before our eyes, with his merits, his defects, his plans, his intentions exposed on his surface, like a garden at which we gaze through a railing, but is a shadow which we can never succeed in penetrating, of which there can be no such thing as direct knowledge, with respect to which we form countless beliefs, based upon his words and sometimes upon his actions, though neither words nor actions can give us anything but inadequate and as it proves contradictory information.

MARCEL PROUST, *Remembrance of Things Past,*
*The Guermantes Way*


In common life don't you often judge and misjudge a man's whole conduct, setting out from a wrong impression? The tone of a voice, a word said in joke, or a trifle in behavior, the cut of his hair or the tie of his neckcloth, may disfigure him in your eyes, or poison your good opinion; or at the end of years of intimacy it may be your closest friend says something, reveals something which had previously been a secret, which alters all your views about him, and shows that he has been acting on quite a different motive to that which you fancied you knew. And if it is so with those you know, how much more with those you don't know?

WILLIAM MAKEPEACE THACKERAY, *The English Humorists*


A man named Lynch told Max Beerbohm that he wished to write his biography. The diminutive Max replied: "My gifts are small. My reputation is a frail plant. Don't over-attend to it, gardener Lynch! Don't drench and deluge it! The contents of a quite small watering can will be quite enough. I find much reassurance and comfort in your phrase, a *little* book. Oh, keep it little!—in due proportion to its theme."

DAVID CECIL, *Max*

# CONTENTS

*Preface*    *xi*
*Acknowledgments*    *xiii*

ONE
Names    1

TWO
History    12

THREE
Gambling    21

FOUR
Jockeys    31

FIVE
California    47

SIX
Forward Seat    58

SEVEN
## Gay Nineties   71

EIGHT
## Mastery   83

NINE
## England   97

TEN
## Monkey Seat   106

ELEVEN
## Yankee Doodle   121

TWELVE
## Trouble   136

THIRTEEN
## Judgment   153

FOURTEEN
## The Wizard   167

FIFTEEN
## Stories   183

*Notes   201*
*Bibliography   213*
*Index   217*

# PREFACE

hy might anyone wish to read about the little antihero of this book? I offer some possible reasons. Tod Sloan was a genius in his line of work, riding thoroughbreds, and took part in and popularized a change in it that overturned two hundred years of tradition.

People have become famous for doing less. That innovation was an important element in the transformation of horse racing into a large-scale twentieth-century business, the first American spectator sport to become a national form of entertainment. Tod Sloan's life opens a small but unusual window onto the popular culture of his day, in which countless people like him (but of course anonymous, as he was not) worked and played, allowing us to learn something about those activities and the attitudes associated with rules and laws, honesty and cheating, success and failure. His career reminds us how inextricably we all live in time, which we experience as change, often unbidden and resisted, always inescapable, and remember as history, shadowy and ambiguous, constantly being revised, but which is real and has consequences. Tod Sloan represented the future but couldn't free himself from the past, from the old ways in which he grew up. So eventually there was no place for him in the horse racing order he helped to inaugurate. Is this too great a weight of significance to put in his cultural saddlebags? I hope not. But that is the reader's call.

# Acknowledgments

"There seems to be hardly anyone among my acquaintance from whom I have not learned." Professor Walter Dubler read an early version of this manuscript in his characteristically generous and informed manner and Dick Painter read a late version in the same spirit. Professor Melanie Mayer was resourceful in finding valuable references. I wish to thank Henry Cohen for conversations about English racing, and Gillian Nutkins, secretary to the director of public affairs, the Jockey Club, London, for the quotation from its "minutes Book." Colleagues in Cowell College and American studies, too numerous to name, have been steadily supportive, as have the University of California, Santa Cruz, staff at the Interlibrary Loan Office, Cowell Faculty Services, Photographic Services, and the Microfilm Archive. Above all, thanks to Henrietta Brown and Cheryl Van De Veer of the Document Publishing and Editing Center. For help with the illustrations, thanks to Simon Eliot, Special Collections, Young Research Library, University of California, Los Angeles; Judy Grunwald, Blood-Horse Publication, Lexington, Kentucky; Field Horne, curator of collections, National Museum of Racing, Saratoga Springs, New York; Barbara Natanson, Photographs Division, Library of Congress; Phyllis Rogers, librarian, Keeneland Association, Keeneland, Kentucky; Sandy Snider, Los Angeles County Arboretum; Emily Wolff, Photography Collection, California Historial Society. Thanks, too, to Tom Wallace of T. C. Wallace, Ltd. Yale University Press conferred two editors upon me: Heidi Downey, who corrected my manuscript with formidable skill and unrelenting care; and Harry Haskell, adviser and friend, as well as editor. Finally, Ann Dizikes brought to reading the manuscript the same aesthetic imagination she lavishes on her beautiful weaving.

# ONE

# NAMES

Names. Tod Sloan had a lot of names (and very little of anything else). His father, cruelly, called him "Toad" because he was so small. His real name, "that which I was christened by," was James Forman Sloan. There was a grander version, too, James Todhunter Sloan, which someone, "I forget who," hung on him. It turned out to be important because it was eventually shortened to Tod, the name everyone called him by. For a number of years he even had a different last name—Blauser—the name of the people who raised him as a boy.

His upbringing was as random as his names, marked by the casual harshness of the lives of ordinary people of the time and place, Bunker Hill, Indiana, twelves miles from Kokomo, where he was born on August 10, 1874. Tod's father had moved there after serving in the northern army during the Civil War; and made his living as a barber and real estate agent, shaving his neighbors both ways. When Tod was five, his mother died. In his own book, *Tod Sloan by Himself,* written long after these events and far away from these places, he said nothing about it, other than to record it. And he said nothing about what happened to the rest of his family—he had two older brothers and a sister—after it occurred. He didn't even mention his mother's name or explain why he had been given to the Blausers. Maybe he didn't know. His history in these years, so obscure to us, may have been equally unknown to him.

*Tod Sloan by Himself* is the source of most of what we know about his early years; its tone is noncommittal about the stories put in, and the ones left out. It is matter-of-fact, offhand, poker-faced, "imperturbable as a gravestone," the style adopted by sportsmen of the time. In its pages the pains of childhood and youth are unrecalled, though very occasionally something deeper flashes out, as in the simple reference to being farmed out to the Blausers "when I was left alone by those I have never ceased to grieve for." A lament for the dead mother, surely, but also for the father who abandoned him? Anyway, that event fixed the pattern of how he perceived his relation to the world: a little guy, on his own, calculating the odds, taking his chances. Tod Sloan, alone, Tod Sloan, by himself.[1]

With the Blausers, however, Tod apparently lived a life that reflected one of the prevailing American cultural archetypes, that of a carefree childhood lived in harmony with nature. This idea, at least as old as the Greeks and Romans, had been given renewed vitality by the Romantic movement of the early nineteenth century, with its emphasis on the innocence of childhood as contrasted with the corruption of social institutions. It wasn't only Americans who invested nostalgic capital in this idea, but it flowered with special luxuriance in the United States because of the nation's recent experience of wilderness and frontier. In the 1870s and 1880s, when Tod was growing up, artists of all kinds illustrated this theme. Winslow Homer painted carefree children frolicking in the fields and meadows, released from captivity in the one-room schoolhouse. James Whitcomb Riley evoked this Hoosier idyll of blameless boys roaming the countryside and sharing innocent amusements. Thomas Bailey Aldrich's novel of 1888, *The Story of a Bad Boy,* was a bestseller. (He wasn't really bad, just mischievous.) This idyllic picture of childhood was only half the story, however. There was also a harshly antiromantic view. In a popular form it was to be found in George W. Peck's bestseller *Peck's Bad Boy and His Pa.* Hennery Peck, the boy, was mean-spirited and sometimes brutal in dealing with parents and peers. He was truly and naturally bad.

Behind and well beyond the imaginative grasp of either James Whitcomb Riley or of George Peck was Mark Twain's vision, in *The Adventures of Tom Sawyer* (1876) and *The Adventures of Huckleberry Finn* (1884), which combined elements of both these views. Twain mordantly depicted the depravity of both young and old in the slaveholding civilization on the riverbanks. But he also captured the freedom, or at least the dream of freedom, to be found in a life in nature, on the Mississippi. Much of the novels' beguiling power rests on their rapturous evocation of life beyond the constraints of the culture.

> Huckleberry came and went at his own free will. He slept on doorsteps in fine weather, and in empty hogsheads in wet; he did not have to go to school or to church, or call any being master, or obey anybody; he could go fishing or swimming when and where he chose, and stay as long as it suited him; nobody forbade him to fight; he could sit up as late as he pleased; he was always the first boy that went barefoot in the spring and the last to resume leather in the fall; he never had to wash, nor put on clean clothes; he could swear wonderfully. In a word, everything that goes to make life precious, that boy had.[2]

Authority could be, must be, deceived and evaded. When the pressures of encroaching culture proved intolerable, Twain's young men survived by tricking people, Tom Sawyer's way, or by running away, Huck's. But no one could run away forever; it never crossed Hennery Peck's mind to try it. And Twain, sometimes reluctantly and always with difficulty, was realistic; whether in the territories of the West or on the mighty river, life was lived within society.

All his life Tod Sloan combined Tom and Huck. In his early years he was Huck. Roaming the Indiana countryside with his dog Tony, he stayed away from school, took up smoking, became "crazy for firearms of all kinds," a passion he couldn't gratify until he was older because in those unenlightened days guns were not readily available to everyone. "I would go out in the fields with Tony and fish, fish, all day long." At other times he was Tom, tricking fellows older and bigger than he was, learning what he could get away with. "Sometimes I got near getting a licking, but I suppose I was too small for them to take very seriously, although I could sting them a bit with my tongue, which was bitter even then." (He always could talk, and one day he would dictate a book.) Later, there were stories that portray him as less a victim of size and circumstance, less innocent. It was said that by age nine he was already fond of man-sized cigars, that "his exploits and adventures knew no limit," that he preferred the company of grown men, that "nothing was too dangerous for him to attempt."[3]

The Blausers put an end to this freedom by threatening him with school. Todd sought refuge twenty miles away, "with my real mother's sister." His aunt let him stay with her for a day or two, but "she kept putting questions, asking me this, that and the other about my schooling and what I was going to do for a living." It was the Widow Douglas civilizing Huck. "She was a good church-woman and never could hold with my not being the same as all the other folk she knew." Tod wasn't the same, and never could be. So he trailed back to the Blausers' house only to find that he couldn't come home again. He had no home. Mrs. Blauser, "without letting me in the front door," asked "whether

I had come for my trunk." Tod, who had no trunk and barely enough clothes to fill a small bag, got the point. "There was no question the situation spelt w-o-r-k." At age thirteen, Tod Sloan hit the road. He was on his own.[4]

After leaving Kokomo, Tod had to be Tom Sawyer, calculating the odds, cutting corners, scrambling to survive. James Whitcomb Riley didn't sing idylls about this Indiana. Gone was harmony with nature. Gone was childhood. (Adolescence hadn't been invented yet.) Soon to go was innocence. Their place was taken, abruptly, shockingly, by learning from the experience of ordinary daily life. Tod went to work in the nearby gas and oil fields, was injured in two explosions, treating his burns with linseed oil and lime water, which "seemed to shrivel me even smaller than I was before." He went back to Kokomo and did a "sort of general utility turn" in a livery stable but was fired because he was so puny. "Although I was willing enough they were always telling me about my helplessness." He looked up his real father, who was now living near Marion, Indiana, and had a new family, but his father did nothing for him. He was unwilling, or too poor, or both. Work turned up in a carriage factory for a while, then in a saloon—sweeping up, attending to the glasses, learning new swear words from the customers. "But it was the same old cry— 'too small,'" so he had to beat it from there. "It was a bit of a knock-out for I used to put in a lot of elbow and wrist work for what my back couldn't do."[5]

Family (and nonfamily), local culture, class, poverty, all these institutions and social conditions were working on Tod Sloan in his wanderings. Nevertheless, the most important thing he had to learn to deal with in these years didn't come through experience or observation and was dictated by nature, not society: his size. Fully grown, he was under five feet in height. He weighed fifty or sixty pounds as he was growing up; in his twenties he weighed about ninety pounds. He wasn't a dwarf; he wasn't ill or disabled. But his small size was inescapable. There were some obvious roles for a very small man: he could work in a circus, become an entertainer, ride horses. In Tod's day there was the historical memory of Napoleon, diminutive but immensely powerful, and of Stephen A. Douglas, the "little giant," Abraham Lincoln's rival from nearby Illinois. Small consolation. What life made clear was that little people had always to look up, and had better look out, for themselves.

In his meanderings Tod met "Professor" A. L. Talbot, a balloonist, a self-described aeronaut, who traveled about the countryside with various sideshows. He was a bit of a con man—the identification of the title professor with something bogus was a persistent aspect of nineteenth-century American culture. But Talbot saw more in Tod than anyone else ever had, so Tod joined up and went along with him. When balloon ascensions didn't draw, the two of them hustled to earn their keep by making toy balloons, which Tod sold. "I tell you I was some salesman, and often think I could have managed a department store if father had taken me by the back of the neck and forced me into business." Tod might indeed have made a good salesman. Words never failed him. Salesmen—"drummers" they were called— epitomized the aggressive, slyly knowing, corner-cutting, and dealmaking commercial culture of the time. An American journalist of the 1890s described these graduates of the Drummers' University, the school of hard knocks: "They know all stories, all jokes, all railroad routes, all hotels, all trades, all games. They are afraid of nothing. They take chances and jump at every opportunity."[6]

Tod Sloan learned his lessons about life from the harsh, shadowy culture of the fast-talking salesman, the carnival pitchman, and the racetrack tout, always on the make, always on the move, legal but essentially furtive. It was a culture of illusion, of sleight-of-hand, of trickery, of seeming more than being. It eluded neat categories of class. It was too occasional and improvised for the discipline of working-class industrial routine; it was entrepreneurial and wholly dependent on the market, but too disreputable, in its commonest forms, to be middle class. Those who were part of it were disdainful of the pieties of middle-class morality and in many ways hostile to the established order because their success depended on beating the system. But they resisted collaboration and were arch individualists, prizing anonymity.

Get-rich-quick-and-easy, something-for-nothing, and taking-a-chance were the prevailing goals of the carnival, the racetrack, the dreams of the salesman. An American gambler believed that the average American was especially susceptible to the wiles of the con man and gambler because of his materialism and cupidity, his "insatiable greed for money, more money. The American eats with it, sleeps with it, dreams of it and lives with it. It is money, money all the time. Go to him with any proposition that has the least bit of plausibility and he will rush to it with the ardor of a boy coasting down hill on the snow." It was a culture essentially Calvinist. In a culture of original sinners, in which everyone was out to trick everyone, there was no sympathy for a victim, only contempt. Given its assumptions about human nature, there was a fitness in cheating the gullible. Joe Weil, a famous con man and swindler known as the Yellow Kid, insisted that "honest men do not exist." "I have never cheated any honest men," he said, "only rascals. They wanted something for nothing. I gave them nothing for something."[7]

Tod Sloan accepted this world. In his memoirs he admitted mistakes but didn't blame himself or others. But for all the matter-of-fact amorality of his narrative, there was in it, between the lines, a vulnerable yearning for a different way, for guidance. Tod Sloan was looking for someone older, wiser, bigger, who would take care of him, set him straight. Professor Talbot was the first of the men whom, in later years, he would identify with his needs. "We were quite a happy family with Talbot." The professor had done a lot of things. He had ridden as a jockey, performed as a clown in the circus, exhibited his equestrian skill by riding two horses, bareback, at the same time. The combative professor fought on the slightest provocation, scrapped for the love of it. Tod later concluded that he hadn't had a hot temper until he met Talbot, whose love of fighting sparked his own. Talbot brawled but never talked about his brawls. Anyone hustling for a living learned to keep his own counsel, to give nothing away. Talking was all right when it was just another way of disguising what was really going on. Talbot explained nothing—about himself, who he was, where he came from, where and how he grew up. A. L. Talbot had no history, only a past. In this he is like the innumerable others who left no records, dictated no books, belonged to nothing, cheated when they could, worked as they had to, and survived.

Once, near Cullum, Indiana, they were heating up for an ascension. Talbot couldn't always get gas, and when he could it often cost too much. So he inflated his balloons in the original way, with hot air. Tod's job was to pile the pine logs and oil barrel staves that were burned to get enough hot vapor to fill the balloon for takeoff. On this occasion Tod saw flames burst out just as the other men on the ground were letting the balloon, and the professor, loose. "Don't go," Tod shouted, but it was too noisy for Talbot to hear him and "with the extra heat he went up all the quicker . . . and I never thought I should see him alive again." At about fifteen hundred feet the balloon was fully on fire; it then collapsed, and the professor came down even quicker than he'd gone up, landing in a field. Somehow the scraps of the balloon's framework broke his fall; Talbot wasn't hurt, only knocked out. He was revived, taken round to a drugstore, and given a shot of brandy. "He got up about an hour after and went to a dance." The professor was tough.

For the Boonesville, Indiana, fair, Talbot came up with a big new idea. He was paid an extra twenty-five dollars for promising a parachute act in connection with the conventional ascension. A boy would slip out of the balloon in a parachute. (Talbot had never seen a parachute, but he got a picture of one and copied it.) One morning he sprang his plan on Tod, who asked:

"Who's the boy?"

"You're the boy."

"Oh, I am!"

"You don't seem to like it, Tod."

"It's all right. But what sort of thing is the para-chute, the umbrella thing I am to come down in? Shall I be heavy enough to make it open out?"

"Oh, you'll be all right," said the Professor, just as if he were saying "Pass the butter," but I began think-ing it over and the more I looked up at the sky and be-gan to think of having to slip down from the clouds the less I liked it.

Tod began to think how he could get out of it. Sometime before this he had learned that his brother Cassius, "Cash," was in the neighborhood. So he told the professor that he wanted to leave. Talbot was sporting about it. "Perhaps you're right; go and join your brother." That was the last they saw of each other.[8]

Tod set out to look for Cash and eventually found him. "I saw a little fellow ahead of me, hiking a mile down a railroad track as hot as a furnace, carrying a pail of water in each hand. He had a long, peaked trotting driver's cap on, and looked the funniest guy I'd ever seen. I walked up behind him to see who he was, and I heard him whistling—and then, of course, I knew it was Cash. We embraced like brothers should. I was glad to see him and he me. We sat down by the track and talked things out."

Cash was a jockey for a stable of horses near St. Louis, and he put Tod to work doing odd jobs. He learned how to rub down horses, to feed and care for them. Work around stables was often dirty, but it wasn't hard. The next step was to become an exercise boy, riding horses to warm them up, then to become a jockey, like Cash. The problem for stable boys who wanted to become jockeys was in getting a chance to ride and gain experience. There was no formal schooling, no apprenticeship; boys learned if they were quick-witted and observant, watching, watching what the others did. Tod's size made him a natural candidate as a featherweight jockey. But there was a special problem. Horses terrified Tod Sloan. He said that his fear of them was connected with a childhood incident; at a funeral he had climbed up on a horse that ran away, out of control. Death and horses got mixed up in his mind. He tried to shake off this fear when working with Cash, but every time he mounted a horse he got thrown, which only made things worse. He hated the whole thing. Still, he reminded himself that trying to ride horses was better than jumping from a balloon; he still had balloon nightmares, "dropping down from the sky with a parachute just out of clutching distance."

Then Cash lost his job with the stable. The two brothers knocked around for a while, moving from place to place, ending up in Denver, where Tod tried riding again, only to be thrown once more. He kept trying because there wasn't anything else. When he was fourteen he and Cash went to Chicago, staying with their sister. Cash supported them by working as a carpenter and, on weekends, as a barber. "Of course little Tod couldn't be out of it," and he helped his brother by standing on a stool and putting in "some fine fancy work," lathering the faces of Cash's customers. In Kansas City he worked for a trainer named Jimmy Campbell, a kindly soul who insisted that Tod could become a success as a rider. Campbell took him east, to New Jersey, where he had his first glimpse of eastern racing. With Campbell's help he began to do what was necessary to overcome his fear—to understand horses. Tod's (or Campbell's) guiding insight was that horses "didn't want to be bullied." It was no good kicking and pulling at them. A rider had to find out each horse's peculiarities and then play up to them. This worked especially well with horses that had a reputation for being bad tempered and sulky. Tod's way with such a horse was Tom Sawyer's way with people; in the struggle between horse and rider for control it was necessary to fool the horse. "I would tug at his bridle a bit then I would relax. That made him think I had given it up—the struggle I mean—and he would strike out for all he was worth under the impression that he'd conquered me." Such a horse then did his best— *"on his own account."*

So Tod started riding professionally. There are differing accounts about when this occurred. In one, "enamored of the turf and the sight of billowing silks," he haunted the barns and stables of a track in St. Louis and got his first mount in 1890. The editor of his memories, who ought to have known, wrote that Sloan "made the acquaintance of race horses in 1886," whatever that might mean. Sam Hildreth, later a notable trainer, encountered Tod in 1886, at the Latonia, Kentucky, racetrack; he was twelve and weighed sixty pounds. "He reminded you of a midget as he squatted on a horse's back." Hildreth gave him a mount, and though Tod's horse "finished nowhere," he handled himself well. Tod remembered his first race as in New Orleans, on Lovelace; he finished third, rode in four other races, and was out of the money in all of them. "If a man didn't want his horse to win, all he had to do was to send for Sloan." No doubt he exaggerated, consciously or not; it made his rise to fame more dramatic. But other people's accounts do suggest that he was not exaggerating when he wrote that "I hated myself for I didn't seem to improve at all." Tod was certainly not precocious. His vagrant rovings in these years— St. Louis, Chicago, New Orleans, a brief eastern visit—are the fitful gropings of someone trying to find his way. He insisted that he had decided to give up riding but was dissuaded by words that kept ringing mysteriously in his ears: "You may be able to ride some day."[9]

And then, in 1892 or 1893, he went to northern California for the winter racing, and that day came.

# TWO

# HISTORY

The horse racing culture Tod Sloan hoped to enter had a long history. Formal horse racing, in the British colonies of North America, dated from the late seventeenth century in New York, the Middle Atlantic Region, and the South. (New England prohibited it as an immoral and frivolous amusement.) The rough, improvised, scattered racing of this founding period gave way to more settled forms in the eighteenth century. Racing clubs were founded and rules and regulations established, though all racing activity remained modest in scale and meager in material resources. From the beginning, two aspects of American racing were fixed: it was entirely decentralized, with little order or uniformity; and everything about it was modeled on English practice.

The Revolutionary War interrupted horse racing but didn't seriously alter the course of its development. The war's greatest effect was psychological.

People came to believe that it had destroyed a golden age of racing when the sport had been in the hands of a high-minded "aristocracy" who sought to improve the breed rather than to gamble and make money. In fact, there wasn't any aristocracy in the English or European sense; there was only a middle class with aristocratic dreams and pretensions. The revolutionary struggle didn't infect American horse racing with the spirit of commercialism; horse raising and horse racing had always been commercial activities. In the absence of a landowning class of inherited wealth, possessing surplus capital and leisure to invest in expensive horses and facilities, it couldn't have been otherwise. But the dream of a golden age haunted American racing, especially in the South, as did the dream of replicating English forms and ways. Tod Sloan's career would be a modest chapter in this transatlantic story.

In the years after national independence, important changes took place in American racing. Larger numbers of English thoroughbreds were imported, and greater emphasis was placed on pedigree. Race horses were more sharply differentiated from work horses. (The democratic impulse found expression in quarter-horse racing, a popular backwoods phenomenon in which pedigree didn't matter at all.) The 1790s and after were a time of expansion. Tennessee, Louisiana, and Kentucky were added to the older centers of racing, though New York remained the actual hub of activity. Expansion was accompanied by wild gambling, speculation, and fraud, and this produced revulsion in the North; horse racing was prohibited in New York for a number of years after 1800. This was the first of a series of cycles of unregulated activity followed by prohibition, then removal of restrictions, followed once again by anarchy, that marked American horse racing culture throughout the nineteenth century and into the twentieth. How to account for this? These cycles were part of a larger cultural pattern, the emergence of the capitalist marketplace as the determinant of value. Hostility to mercantilist paternalism, antagonism to government, opposition to regulation of almost any sort—these expressed the prevailing public philosophy. The actual results of that philosophy were disquieting, however, because unregulated competition in horse racing led not to honesty but to the reverse.

In the 1820s horse racing was revived in New York, once again with a minimum of regulatory supervision. The number of race meetings and race horses increased, as did the amount of money invested in facilities and horses. Jockey clubs sprang up, modeled on the great original in Newmarket, England (or so the members hoped); nomenclature and rules, so far as they existed, were drawn from the same source. But the form of racing remained what it had been in the eighteenth century. Races were brutally exhausting, two or three miles, two out of three or three out of five heats. It was not uncommon for horses to race fifteen miles in a day. (This was possible only because the pace was very slow.) Stamina—"bottom," they called it—was far more important than speed. The race was against other horses, not against the clock; in fact, the English didn't usually bother to record the elapsed time of a race. Ironically, this old style of racing was going out of fashion in England. Like all provincials, the Americans were more royalist than the king.

Despite the almost hypnotic power of English racing traditions, American racing developed distinctive characteristics. Americans raced on dirt "tracks," not on grass, or "turf," for they lacked the cheap labor and the capital required to maintain turf courses. American race tracks had often been hacked out of the fields and forests taken from the Indians. These were enclosed, and admission was charged. Racing seasons were sporadic, not part of an orderly, long-established social calendar, as in England. Most notably, horse racing in the United States was closely associated with urban culture, even in the South, though the desired image was of its taking place in a pastoral Arcadia. The urban orientation was dictated by the prevailing social structure. Lacking aristocratic patrons of the sport for whom it was to some extent an end in itself or part of the obligations of one's class,

American horse racing, with its market orientation, was dependent on attracting an audience, and this was to be found in sufficient numbers only near cities.

In the first half of the nineteenth century there was one feature of American racing that was unparalleled in England: the North versus South match races, held on the Union Course, Long Island, the nearest thing there was to a national race track. In the first of these, in 1823, Eclipse, the northern horse, defeated Sir Henry in two out of three heats, four miles each. By the time of the last such race, Peytona versus Fashion in 1845, there had been thirty of them. But sectional fervor had become too bitter to be contained by anything as peaceful as a horse race. The Mexican War ended these races and introduced fifteen years of political conflict that culminated in the Civil War.

The most immediate and visible effect of the Civil War was that horse racing was ruined throughout the South, except in Louisiana, Maryland, and Kentucky. Northern preeminence became northern near-monopoly. It wasn't the war only, of course. The expansion of racing that took place in the Ohio Valley, in the Midwest, and in the Pacific states was based on the spectacular growth of the northern and western industrial economies. Racing had always been intensely local, with the exception of the occasional regional match race; now it became truly regional and even national. By using trains, stable owners could transport numbers of horses cheaply, safely, and quickly from one race meeting to another. That had been possible to some extent by the 1850s, but with the completion of the transcontinental railroad in 1869, horses could go from coast to coast. A more urban and cosmopolitan racing culture emerged. But important elements of the old one remained as well, old and deeply ingrained attitudes, traditions that people clung to even as they adapted to new conditions.

One thing new was the appearance on the racing scene of immensely wealthy new capitalists—August Belmont,

D. D. Withers, Leonard Jerome, Pierre Lorillard, William C. Whitney, and many others—who invested far more capital in racing than had even been done before. They built new race tracks adjacent to the large urban centers and within easy reach of railroad lines. Immigrants from Europe enormously swelled the size of cities and increased the potential racing audience; ways eventually had to be found to get these new people to the tracks.

In the meantime, an equal flood of people had moved into the cities from farms and small towns, people already familiar with horses and racing. Capturing their attention and interest was the first order of business. Women had to be induced to attend by making the tracks safer, less rowdy, beautiful. And ladies' days were introduced, with free or partial admission. Attracting the working class was complicated by the problem that work schedules in factories were inflexible. However, much city labor was still casual, piecework labor; craft and domestic workers also had less rigid schedules. Saturday racing became a fixture, and important races were scheduled on that day. Meets were extended over more days in the week and more weeks in the month. By the 1880s California race tracks had two hundred or more racing days a year. In 1890–91, the Gloucester City, New Jersey, track had a continuous 176-day meeting, with races on Christmas and New Year's Day. But the record probably belonged to the 354-day meeting held in 1893 in East St. Louis, Illinois. The demand for horses to fill so many racing dates was greater than the supply, and many horses were raced to the verge of exhaustion. "In fact, it became a survival of the fittest," an American trainer remembered, "and every dodge and device was used to keep the poor devils up to the mark, and some man hit on the marvelous properties of cocaine for the jaded horse."[1]

At the same time, the growth of cities was adding to the instability of racing culture. The urban population gobbled up the land on which the new race tracks were built; the life expectancy of a track was one generation. There was nothing new in the social aspirations of the new capitalists: to legitimize their money and their social climbing by association with the sport of kings, just as their contemporaries patronized opera houses or collected old masters.

The most important of these new race tracks was Jerome Park, in New York. It was an example of the new plutocracy's attempt to "raise horse racing from disrepute to the high standard it obtained in England," an effort to maintain a "royal sport, not rowdies' outings." The Jeromes, of Huguenot ancestry, came to America at the beginning of the eighteenth century but never achieved, or pretended to, any social eminence. Leonard Jerome was born in 1818 in upstate New York, to a farming family. He worked at odd jobs as a young man, attended Princeton for two years but withdrew for lack of money, then finished his education at Union College. He became a lawyer, published a newspaper, was involved in Whig politics, moved to New York City, and eventually made a fortune as a Wall Street speculator. Serving as U. S. consul in Trieste in 1852, and living in Paris in 1858–59, sharpened his taste for opera and horses and gave him a cosmopolitanism unusual among his contemporaries. Not content with a stable of horses and an interest in the Saratoga race track, he aspired to something grander and, with William Travers and August Belmont, organized the American Jockey Club as the instrument for his ambitions.

In 1866 he purchased the Bathgate estate at Fordham, New York. In the middle of the 230-acre property was a large hill, called the Bluff. On this eminence he built the Club-House, before which "the track curled in full view," and across from it, the Grand Stand, seating seven thousand. Jerome Park was celebrated for its opulence. The Club-House had a ballroom, dining rooms, and an art gallery. From a nearby bandstand came the music of Jacques Offenbach, whose operas were then the rage in the city. Open the year round, the Club-House became a rendezvous for society. When it opened, in September 1866 to great fanfare, there were carriages innumerable, and U. S. Grant as

Jerome Park, 1873. The horse Tom Bowling winning the Jerome Stakes. Note the Club-House on the bluff and the conventional riding style of the jockeys. National Museum of Racing, Saratoga Springs, New York.

guest of honor, as well as people who didn't possess a diploma of respectability. In the infield one heard the "babel of different tongues, Italian, German, Irish brogue."[2]

The Saratoga, New York, race track was an influential example of the racing renaissance of the Gilded Age, but it was also an exception to the emerging pattern, combining elements of the racing culture of the past as well as of the future, of the exclusive as well as democratic. Saratoga Springs had for many years been known as a rustic health spa. In the 1860s, gambling helped transform it into a flourishing and cosmopolitan summer resort, a rival to Newport, Rhode Island. As Jerome Park was the American Newmarket, Saratoga was the American Ascot. The man primarily responsible for it was very different from the tycoon type. John Morrissey, who founded his race track in 1863, in the midst of the Civil War, was a champion pugilist, the street-brawling leader of the Dead Rabbits, a Tammany Hall gang, and a member of Congress for a term. The race track (and gambling casino), though a considerable distance from any city, nevertheless drew an urban clientele. Local residents were denied entrance to the red brick casino. Women were welcome to visit its

John Morrissey, pugilist,
gambler, congressman, and
founder of the race track in
Saratoga, New York. Cartoon
by Thomas Nast.

salon and drawing rooms but forbidden the gaming rooms. The
summer visitors were diverse: "Eastern financial titans, Western
bonanza kings, transportation tycoons, statesmen and politicians, society dilettantes, and a swarm of lesser mortals."[3]

Saratoga was the exception. The other new race tracks were
more or less modeled on Jerome Park. In 1870 some Maryland
gentlemen, including Ogden Bowie, the governor of the state,

organized a jockey club and built Pimlico race track near Baltimore; the first stakes race there was won by Preakness, for whom a famous race would be named in later days. After several false starts, San Francisco's Bay District track, opened in 1874, would be the center of California racing. In Kentucky, a new race track, Churchill Downs, opened in 1875. There was extraordinary growth in the Ohio Valley, with dozens of small tracks being built in Ohio, Indiana, and Illinois. The center of midwestern racing was Chicago, where Washington Park opened in 1884; it featured a 1⅛-mile track, the largest in the country at the time, with a concentric track of conventional size in the infield. The American Derby, inaugurated at Washington Park that year, was for some time the richest race in the country. Philip Sheridan was president of the track, and the day the American Derby was run was practically a public holiday in Chicago. New Orleans was the one southern city to reestablish racing after the Civil War. The old Metairie track, the queen of American tracks, closed in 1872, but a new one, the Fair Grounds, opened the same year.

Tod Sloan grew up in a time of extraordinary excitement. Everywhere, horse racing was attracting more and more money.

# THREE

# GAMBLING

Horse racing has always been both a sport and a form of gambling: handsome, high-spirited animals competing against each other and personal wagers made in agreeable circumstances. In the nineteenth century, however, the nature of horse race betting changed. With the appearance of professional gamblers and bookmakers, it became institutionalized; and it became entangled in the law. Both of these things happened first in Great Britain, and their consequences were soon felt in the United States. In 1853, Parliament passed An Act for the Suppression of Betting Houses, which prohibited betting shops or places but allowed betting with bookmakers at race courses. This law couldn't prevent individuals from betting with bookmakers away from race courses, but such bets had to be made surreptitiously. Some of the displaced British bookmakers emigrated to France. In time, the French responded to their presence by in-

venting the mechanical pari-mutuel betting system. Many of the
rest of the British bookmakers left their country for their country's good and came to the United States.

By 1856 an observer noted the presence at American race
tracks of a "huge agglomeration of gambling and fraud . . . of
men whose interest in [racing] is the interest of 'sharps' and 'gamblers.'" Americans had nothing to learn from anyone else about
race track cheating and trickery, but the presence of professional
gamblers on this scale was a new thing. The bookmakers also set
up shops in the larger American cities; in Philadelphia, which led
the way, they offered their professional services for betting on
cricket matches (very popular in the Philadelphia area at mid-
century), rowing regattas, and trotting races. But there and
everywhere else, horse racing became the focus of bookmaking.
Horse racing and bookmaking stimulated each other; gambling
increased the stream of money pouring into horse racing in the
1870s and 1880s, while the growth in the number of tracks,
horses, and races, which this money made possible, also increased the demand for bookmakers. Before the Civil War, the
leading forms of gambling in the United States had been the numerous state lotteries and card and dice games, especially faro
and poker. By the mid-1880s, state lotteries had disappeared,
and horse race gambling surpassed all the other kinds of betting.[1]

There were three ways to bet on horse races in professional
betting. The first was auction pools, the mainstay of the city betting shops, to which reports of the races throughout the country were sent by telegraph from the various tracks. Each horse in
a given race was put up to bid; the highest bidder took the entire
pool if his horse won. The manager of the auction pool took a
percentage of the winnings as his profit. There were a number of
disadvantages to this cumbersome system. No one knew the
odds at which any horse went off. All betting (bidding) was oral
and public. Most significantly, the most favored horse went to
the bidder with the most money, which excluded the average bettor with little money from taking part. The betting shops became

known as "pool" halls because of this type of betting. In the shops billiard tables were provided to afford entertainment to the customers between races. Later, the word "pool" attached itself to some of the cue-and-ball games played there. Later still, when bookmakers replaced auction bidding, pool halls became bookie joints.

The bookmaker represented the second way of betting. His (or her, there were women bookmakers) function was to facilitate betting by taking bets brought to him, while his personal objective was to adjust the odds so that he would profit no matter which horse won. At the race track, bookmakers occupied separate areas known as "rings," which were marked off from the rest of the track; entry was permitted by an admission charge. In California women were generally allowed to pay their fee and enter the betting ring to mingle with the speculators and wager their money; eastern tracks were more virtuous and prohibited women from squandering their money in this way. At most race tracks there were two of these: the metropolitan ring, where the biggest and best-known bookmakers operated, and the field ring, for the smaller bookmakers and bettors. The rings were often on different sides of the race track proper, the field ring being in the infield. Wherever located, the rings were usually roofed but opensided. A big blackboard hanging above each bookmaker's stall bore the names of the horses, with the odds for each; the odds changed according to the bookmaker's calculations. Each bookmaker was able to see the blackboards of his competitors. The bookmaker "made his book," that is, accepted bets, with the help of assistants, sheet writers (recordkeepers), and pay-off men.

For the uninitiated this wagering system was puzzling, noisy, chaotic. Bettors went from bookie to bookie to find the best odds, battled the crowd to get their money into the hands of the bookmaker and his assistants, made sure that the number of the bet was correctly recorded on the bookmaker's sheets. Although the bookkeeping system gave the small individual bettor

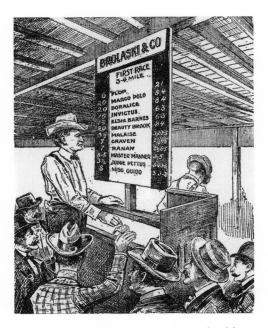

A typical bookmaker of the time, with odds
board. Race track betting was a personal
transaction.

greater latitude in picking and betting on a horse than did auction pool betting, small-time bookies often refused to take bets
if there was too much money on one horse. Nor could they take
large bets; twenty dollars was a substantial bet for the field ring.
By contrast, the metropolitan ring catered to the wealthy and to
the small number of celebrated "plungers," the independent big-
time gamblers, the buccaneers of the race track.

The most publicized of these plungers was John Warne
"Bet-a-Million" Gates, who was born and grew up in Du Page
County, Illinois. His only inheritance was rural poverty, so he
soon "set about the task of abolishing his inheritance." He
husked corn, Tom Sawyer–like, "making plans for capitalizing

the work of the other boys." He became a grain salesman, sold barbed wire in Texas, then manufactured it. He was untroubled by not having patents for what he made and sold; when legal action was taken against him he simply moved his equipment across the nearest state line and went on making and selling. Nocturnally eluding process servers, he was known as Moonshine Gates.

His biographer recognized that "few affirmative lessons can be drawn from the life of this eminently successful Westerner." Racing life was indistinguishable for him from business life. "Business ethics were no part of his practice." When he got into the biggest gambling game in the country, Wall Street, J. P. Morgan immediately distrusted him; Gates didn't play by the rules, Morgan's rules. Gates was not pious, meek, respectable; he smoked and drank, was awed by no authority. Horses interested him only as a way of making money. He placed huge bets, always on the favorite. It was the size of the bet that interested him— and it was that which fascinated the millions who read about him and dreamed of emulating him. Reticence was, for him, only a word in the dictionary. He once hired a man to follow him with a large market basket into which bookmakers dropped the cash they owed him after he had landed a big winner.[2]

The third type of betting was "French pools," or Paris-Mutuels, what came to be known as the pari-mutuel system. In the 1870s Pierre Oller, a Parisian who sold perfumes, lottery tickets, and booked bets, invented a ticket-selling and calculating apparatus that allowed bettors to bet among themselves, in any amount and on any horse. The machine was operated by the race track, which assumed no risk and was neutral as to the transaction, other than to take a small percentage for handling the bet. In its original form the thing consisted of a booth with a ticket seller in front; behind him was a rack of tickets numbered from one to twelve, depending on how many horses were entered in each race. The bettor chose his horse, paid his money, and got his ticket from the seller; a man running a register recorded the bet by tugging a string connected to the matching number on the board. The odds were a function of the total amount of money bet on a given horse as a percentage of the total amount bet on all horses. Pari-mutuel machines were introduced at American tracks in the late 1870s.

The three methods of betting battled for predominance all through the late nineteenth century. Pool rooms could coexist with bookmakers or with pari-mutuel machines at the race track, at least for the short run; they appealed to different customers. Pool hall habitués were there for the gambling; they didn't want to watch the horses run, didn't care to go to the track. The deadly rivalry was between the bookmaking and pari-mutuel systems. Every dollar bet with a machine was a dollar lost to the bookie. This rivalry involved matters more complex than simply how to place a bet, matters at the heart of the horse racing culture that nourished Tod Sloan and whose values he wholeheartedly absorbed.

The machine was an impersonal contrivance, but the bookmaker was an aggressive presence. Bookmakers' survival depended on being able to "reduce the hazards of their trade." Inside information gave them an advantage in calculating odds, so they paid stables for information of all kinds—the state of mind and inclinations of the jockey, the objectives of the trainer and owner, the condition of the horse. They posted their own clerks along the rail for early-morning workouts. They owned horses—"plow horses"—with no chance of winning their races, running at spectacular odds to attract the sucker bettors. But most of all, they interfered directly (but secretly) in the actual racing, influencing jockeys, trainers, and owners.

In fact, bookmakers were the center of much of the corruption at the race track, and everyone knew it. Pierre Lorillard, after many years' experience as an owner, put the case against bookmakers who "rob the public and rob the owners of horses. In the course of plying his trade, [the bookmaker] steals stable secrets and buys up jockeys and trainers." The bookmaking system, Lorillard went on, "is demoralizing and hurtful to every-thing and everybody connected with racing." And he con-cluded—hopefully but wrongly: "We have outlived the neces-sity for these fellows." Several race tracks attempted to get rid of the bookmakers, without success. What were the sources of the bookmakers' power?[3]

Race tracks profited directly from the presence of book-makers, who paid them between $17.50 and $57.50 per day to conduct their business there. But bookmakers were not just im-portant clients, they were powerfully intertwined with the dom-inant groups that managed the race tracks. Many of the leading racing figures of the day were gamblers or had made their money as gamblers. John Morrissey, the founder of the Saratoga race track, had grown up in the intermeshed culture of gambling money and political patronage; his experience was unusual only in its flamboyance. "Old Smoke" Morrissey opened a casino in Saratoga as well. There he conducted the auction pool and gave himself 5 percent of all profits for this service; and there too he sometimes acted as stakeholder for the big plungers who fre-quented his establishment, and who bet as much as $200,000 a day, with Morrissey taking 5 percent of that as well. Louis Cella, who managed race tracks in and around St. Louis, was known for his real estate and theatrical holdings, but his money came primarily from gambling. Barney Schreiber, also a midwesterner, was prominent at northern California tracks in Sloan's heyday there, and owned a stable, but he had begun his racing career as a gambler and continued his gambling even as he ran his horses. There were no rules against this. Gamblers who owned and op-erated casinos took part in organizing Monmouth Park race track at Long Branch, New Jersey. Mike and Phil Dwyer, sons of a butcher, grew up in Brooklyn and gambled heavily at the New York race tracks, amassing enough money to be able to buy their own horses and, in the 1880s, compete with racing's social nabobs. In 1883 the Dwyer stable was said to have won more purse money in one year than any other in the world. In 1886 the Dwyers organized the Brooklyn Jockey Club, with their own race track at Gravesend. The brothers quarreled in 1890 and split up, and Mike formed a partnership with Richard Croker, the Tammany Boss, and continued his very heavy betting.

With time, some of these men came to be thought of as pillars of the established racing order. Such was Edward R. Bradley. Born in Johnstown, Pennsylvania, in 1859, he worked in the Pennsylvania steel mills, went West as a prospector, became a skillful gambler, and then set up as a bookmaker at tracks in the Mississippi Valley. Eventually he gained control of Churchill Downs Race Course in Lexington, Kentucky, and astutely promoted the Kentucky Derby to national prominence. From his celebrated Idle Hour farm came four Derby winners and an estate worth millions, but even when, in the 1920s, he had become the much-venerated "Colonel" Bradley, he continued to own and operate the fashionable Beach Club gambling casino at Palm Beach, Florida.[4]

Anyone seeking to reform race track bookmaking had to contend with the fact that race tracks and city political machines were often closely linked. In Chicago the bookmaking syndicate in the 1880s was under the control of a prominent politician, Michael McDonald; rival syndicates, led by men with such enchanting names as Hinky Dink McKenna and Bath House John Coughlin, challenged his dominance; but whatever their internecine struggles they were united in supporting the bookmaking–race track combination. In New York City, Boss Richard Croker took the offensive and in 1888 got a state law passed that barred pari-mutuel betting. Croker, an avid horse player, bookmaker, and horse owner, and his supporters formed the Metropolitan Turf Association, an exclusive group of high-stakes bookmakers, limited to two hundred members. At one time, in the 1890s, membership in the "Mets" ring cost $7,000, the price of a seat on the New York Stock Exchange at that time.

The line between the gamblers-owners-patrons and the conventional patrons of greater respectability—Jerome and

This caricature of a racing judge makes clear
the futility of efforts to regulate racing.

Withers, Lorillard and Belmont—was not clear cut. The Wall
Street barons used business tactics that were no different from
those displayed every day at the race track. Who could teach
Daniel Drew or Jay Gould any tricks he didn't already know?
Racing and business culture both heartily accepted this golden
rule: "Do unto others what they would do unto me if they had
a chance, and do it first." Polite society recoiled in horror from
John Morrissey, but Commodore Vanderbilt was pleased to race
his trotters against Morrissey's in Central Park. And Jerome and
Withers and Belmont and many others helped finance Morrissey's racing and gambling ventures at Saratoga while Morrissey,
who held the controlling interest, remained in the background.

All the money that came into racing from business and
gambling and politics, as Jerome's biographer commented, "lay
in a strange tangle of crude, tough, corrupt circles of power.
Where respectability began and ended did not always distinctly

show." Jerome was no doubt pleased with the estimate of the *New York Times* after opening day: "Nothing goes on at Jerome Park which the purest minded person could object to. There is no bribing of jockeys, no 'dosing' of horses with laudanum. Never did the history of racing in any country begin with so fair a page." But one suspects that he thought it effusive, somewhat naive. Jerome had the reputation of being peculiarly frank and straight in his methods, in business (so far as one knows) and in sport. But he was very worldly. He accepted the world pretty much as he found it, knew how rackets started and flourished, didn't attempt to abolish them, but wished to keep them away from his race track. The gamblers and political bosses were welcome to come to Jerome Park "to gamble and flaunt their mistresses," but he wanted to protect and preserve his "untarnished sportsman's dream. Money must be earned elsewhere." Jerome accepted the adage that "gamblers are good for racing in the way that a certain number of fleas are good for a dog." He would most certainly agree with the estimate of a one-time ("reformed") gambler: "Not one professional gambler in a thousand is at all times absolutely square." But might not a gambler have replied, if he thought it worth his while: Not one Wall Street nabob, not one patron of the turf, not one trainer or judge or jockey, and not one ordinary race goer is, at all times, absolutely square?[5] Both statements are exaggerations. Yet skepticism, not cynicism, was the appropriate point of view, because gambling was not the only cause of uncertainty about what was going on. Much of that uncertainty was inherent in the complex relationship between owners and trainers and the little men in whose hands the reins and the actual running of the race were finally put—the jockeys.

# J O C K E Y S

"A difference of opinion is what makes a horse race," but human intervention in the form of handicapping—weight to equalize differences in natural ability—is what makes horse racing a commercial activity and spectator sport. "A horse race that people will bet on is a horse race that has been handicapped to make it a betting proposition." In seventeenth-century England horses ran under "catch" weights, whatever their amateur riders (often their owners) happened to weigh. In the eighteenth century, as horse racing became a public sport, a series of graduated weights was established according to the age, sex, experience, and quality of each horse. Varying weights necessitated specialized riders; so emerged the professional jockey. Emphasis on speed meant that featherweight jockeys were sought after.

Handicapping horses is based on informed but far from infallible judgment; yet the amount of weight a horse carries is a crucial factor in winning or losing. In 80 percent of races the difference between victory and defeat is one length. The perfectly handicapped race, in which every possible variable would be balanced by assigned weights, producing a dead heat among all contestants, has never been achieved, though there have been dead heats among as many as three horses. In the nineteenth century in the United States, each race track employed a handicapper. Although not a professional, he was someone who knew the horses running in the locality of the track and came to know something about the horses shipped to the track from elsewhere. No doubt there was chicanery involved, but incompetence was a greater problem than dishonesty. If the weights assigned were arbitrary, owners simply withdrew their horses. So it was in the interest of the race track to keep weights within a reasonable range. Even so, weight differentials of thirty and forty pounds were not unknown. Did handicapping work? In England, at least, there is evidence that racing form was leveling out in the 1890s; the percentage of races won by small margins increased and the percentage of favorites winning declined. And the same may well have been true in the United States.

The "difference of opinion" that leads people to bet on a horse race has another meaning. The triangular relationship of owner, trainer, and jockey is saturated in ambiguities. The interests and judgment of the three are not necessarily identical. What the owner wants and expects of his horse may vary from race to race; so, too, the trainer's judgment about what is right for it; and the jockey's sense of this might be different still. Like the trainer, but more visibly, the jockey, even trying his best might not be able to achieve the objectives set for him; less obviously, he might not care to. Anyway, jockeys have traditionally been thought poor pickers of winners. "Any man who follows the advice of his jockey is sure to be ruined." And even when the judgments and interests of the three are perfectly matched and the horse cooperates, racing luck may undo everything. "Yet, notwithstanding the difficulties with which the subject is beset, it is one on which everyone with five minutes so-called experience speaks with authority. Then if their opinion should chance to be upset they at once proceed to assail jockeys, trainers and owners, when nothing is at fault save their own judgment."[1]

Famous and wealthy owners appear prominently in these pages, but of the most common type of owner—the small businessman working in an age of larger and larger enterprises, the independent owner of modest means, with a horse or two, who lived on the margins of the racing scene, who struggled against bad luck, crooked competition, prevailing trickery—we know little. They might be represented by the California owner T. H. Ryan, of whom it was said: "His horses, run honestly all the time, win at any and all prices, and he backs them no matter what the odds." There was a stinger in the tail of this tribute. "His methods must be a revelation to a great many California owners."[2]

Trainers, as variable in type and morals as owners or jockeys, occupied the intermediate position in the racing hierarchy. We know much less about them than about owners and jockeys. The trainer's authority, great within the stable, was a good deal less clear in regard to the owner and jockey. Most American trainers came into the sport through the direct experience of horse raising and racing and through family connections. There had to be money to get started; trainers usually charged a weekly or monthly fee for their services, but owners did not always meet their payments or were late in doing so. As horse racing became a bigger business, the status of trainers increased; by the end of the nineteenth century a few—James Rowe, Sam Hildreth, John E. Madden—became well known in their own right, and this would accelerate in the twentieth century.

How honest were trainers? There were no prohibitions against their betting on races except for betting against their own horses. Trainers had usually to depend on others—jockeys or stable boys—to do their dirty work if they had that in mind; trainers often felt betrayed by jockeys in the way a race was run, though they too could not always tell whether a loss was due to malice or incompetence. Ed Corrigan, a leading California owner-trainer, was "very much put out" at the way Tod Sloan rode Moblaska, opening out at so killing a pace that the horse tired, was overtaken, and then beaten, though "easily a better animal than the winner." Even Corrigan, a knowledgeable and worldly racing figure, might never have figured out what was going on. Only in regard to doping horses could the trainer act on his own. No doubt there were numerous jockeys who, when mounting a horse, found that *they* had been betrayed. Owners, too. James R. Keene wanted to race his horse Sysonby in England, but his trainer, the widely admired James Rowe, wished to keep it in the American stable. When Sysonby was brought out for inspection Rowe had it so heavily blanketed and bandaged that Keene decided it was not fit to be sent abroad. In fact, Sysonby was in perfect condition.[3]

The general public, and certainly bettors, judged a trainer's skill as they did any jockey's, by the number of winners he saddled. At best this was an imperfect standard. A trainer often raced a horse he knew was not yet fit but needed the race as conditioning. If bettors didn't understand this, it was their lookout. Conversely, a horse brought to peak condition might be held back for various reasons. And then there was the inexorable law of handicapping: victories and increased weight reduced the odds of winning again. It would seem a truism that preparing a horse to run was the hallmark of a good trainer. But this, too, was disputed. A different point of view was that the trainer's "greatest skill is not in getting a horse ready to run—almost all follow the same methods for this—but in placing his horse in a race in which it has an advantage not perceived by others." Of innumerable instances of the variability and ambiguity of performance, take that afforded by a horse called The Winner, which ran "an extremely bad race; the general opinion was to the effect that [the horse] was not fit for a hard race and should not have been started." The trainer came before track authorities, and the betting sheets of prominent gamblers were examined. Nothing came of it. Many trainers believed that actual racing experience was more important than nonracing workouts. If The Winner did well the next time out, might that only have demonstrated that it needed the previous race to get into winning form?[4]

And then there were the jockeys. The word originally was a diminutive of John or Jock and was applied to any man of the common people—to minstrels, beggars, or vagabonds. By the seventeenth century it was associated with horse dealers and was a synonym for sharp practice. Jocking or jockeying a man meant tricking or cheating him, and as horse riding emerged as a profession, riders came to be called jocks or jockeys and to be associated with combativeness and deceit.

In the United States there was no apprenticeship training for jockeys, as there was in Great Britain and on the Continent. Jockeys came from the bottom of the social heap; they were often runaways, orphans, impoverished, and uneducated. For most of them the race rack and its stables were not only work but a home of sorts. Constantly on the move, these boy-men lived precarious lives, vulnerable to the demands and desires of the trainers and owners who employed them. They were often homeless, often fatherless; some had fathers who were indifferent, perhaps exploitive, brutal. No wonder they learned to trick and deceive. And no wonder they were often wrathful and explosive. Their combativeness was frequently emphasized. "The bantam rooster is traditionally the most truculent fowl in the barnyard, and the breed of Little Men has never been noted for its modesty." Or its passivity. Horse racing is dangerous, and riding the most dangerous task of all; most races are won by aggressive riding. Fights among jockeys were common and stabbings were not unknown.[5]

Professional jockeys generally were very small, and in the United States in the late nineteenth century, they were getting smaller. The steady movement toward shorter races, with a premium placed on speed, meant that featherweight riders were

Weighing the jockeys.

more sought after than ever. To gain weight was for most jockeys to lose their distinctive attribute, so they were faced with continual sweating in Turkish baths or with strict diet. Isaac Murphy was an extraordinary man and rider in every respect except one: he fought a lifelong battle against the jockey's curse, weight gain. When he ate normally his weight went up to 130 to 135 pounds. He died of pneumonia at age thirty-seven, possibly weakened by enforced dieting and sweating in steam baths. Drinking was as common among jockeys as was rowdiness; drunken jockeys were a familiar sight. Their drinking was closely connected with fear of gaining weight; alcohol, jockeys believed, was a form of weightless sustenance. Isaac Murphy drank champagne to gain strength, and, in the last few years of his life, was an alcoholic.[6]

The turbulence of jockey culture increased in the 1890s because of racial conflicts. This was the decade in which overt social segregation between blacks and whites was given legal sanction in *Plessy vs. Ferguson,* the decisive Supreme Court decision of 1896. The last years of the 1890s and the first decade of the twentieth century saw the crushing imposition, nationally, of social segregation by means of lynching and other forms of brutality. At the same time, and for several reasons, more white featherweights entered racing. The purses for winning races increased steadily. Opportunities for African-American stable boys at the small tracks declined, which meant that it was harder for them to get into racing at all. Within a few years they were systematically excluded. A few African-American trainers—Ed Brown, Albert Cooper, and others—had been successful and highly regarded, but by the end of the century, African-American trainers, too, were excluded.

The prospects of all African-American jockeys diminished as well. The fortunes of Willie Simms, one of the leading jockeys of the decade, declined sharply. "I did not seem able to get mounts [in America] which had any reasonable chance of winning," he reported; so in 1900 and 1901 he raced in France. The owners of the horses and of the race tracks turned a blind eye to what was happening, if in fact they didn't support driving African-American jockeys off the tracks. There were exceptions. In June 1895 the board of stewards of the Bay District track in San Francisco "took cognizance" of what had been obvious to many observers, a conspiracy to defeat the African-American jockey Chevalier; he had been crowded and cut off continually, systematically interfered with. All the jockeys were given a warning. The interference went on anyway.[7] As far as one can tell, Tod Sloan shared the feelings of the other white jockeys. Though he had an African-American servant who traveled with him for many years, he never expressed any criticism of what was going on and in his memoirs casually referred to his white valet at the track and his "nigger" valet in town.

Sloan's road to racing was neither harsher nor easier than that of many others. We can trace something of the lives of his generation of jockeys through the career of Bill "Father" Daly (1837–1931), a trainer of horses and young men, among them some of the most famous riders in American racing—Edward "Snapper" Garrison, Fred Taral, Jimmy McLaughlin, Danny Maher, Winnie O'Connor. A stone quarry worker and bartender, Daly, whose long life suggest that the bad die old, combined sadism and paternalism in his treatment of his boys. He beat them with barrel staves and they beat their horses, for Daly taught the use of the whip. Father Bill was rough, Winnie O'Connor wrote, "but he made us all rich. The only thing he didn't teach us was how to save our money."

O'Connor was born in Brooklyn in 1884. His path to riding was urban, in contrast to Tod Sloan's rural one. O'Connor, who "never got beyond the first school reader," was enchanted by the huge brewery horses that pulled wagons with kegs of beer through the streets of Brooklyn. He ran away from home at age ten, weighing forty-five pounds, and found his way to the Brighton Beach race track, where he approached Big Mike Daly, Bill's brother and also a trainer. Winnie asked him if he could learn about horses.

"Got any parents?" Big Mike asked.

"'Not with me,' I answered truthfully."

"Can't take kids without the consent of parents." New York state had passed a law to protect boys from this kind of exploitation. O'Connor's grandfather eventually vouched for him and Big Mike took him on, paying Winnie's parents $25 for his first year with him, $50 for the second, $100 for the third.[8]

Few other states had such laws; or if they did have, they were frequently ignored. Witness the case of a young jockey named Smoky Taylor. He had been riding for some years for an owner who laid claim to the boy's services on the basis of some "guardianship" papers in his possession. Taylor's entire pay for his riding was one suit of clothes, "only that and nothing more." Not surprisingly, Taylor ran away from this "home." His guardian went to court to secure an injunction to prevent Taylor from riding for anyone else. When the case came to trial, evidence was presented that Taylor, an orphan, had been subjected to physical mistreatment; he reported "some rough stories about his employer." The judge was scathing. "The days of slavery are past, I believe. You [the guardian] have committed an outrage. The idea that an orphan should be farmed out for a suit of clothes is simply infamous. The boy has earned as much as $300 a day and I cannot sufficiently condemn the conduct of his assumed guardian." But for every outraged judge there were numerous exploited Taylors.[9]

Bill Daly taught his boys how to feed and care for horses, how to saddle them, to be "soft-handed" with them, how to win their confidence. "It wasn't all pink teas, gals and booze parties." He smacked his pupils without apology. Some left him; one threatened him with a pistol. But many others gave him fierce, unquestioned loyalty. O'Connor was scathing about those who would reform things. "Just imagine the chorus of modern sob sisters, if anything like that was pulled off today . . . the women's clubs would let out a yell and the Parent-Teacher Associations would pass resolutions and there'd be speeches in the legislature."[10] No doubt we think his sarcasm misplaced. But from O'Connor's point of view that loyalty was yielded to Daly as to one's father.

As a young man in Indiana, Tod encountered the example represented by the combative Professor Talbot. Winnie O'Connor also liked to fight, with gloves or without. The way he chose to be reconciled with his father, from whom he had run away, was to arrange to fight, in his father's presence, with an obliging local newsboy named Jimmy Crow. By this point in his life O'Connor had learned a trick or two; as insurance, he paid Crow $50 to throw the fight. It was agreed that O'Connor would knock out Crow in the first round. "That wasn't sporting but I did it." Once the fight began, however, not only wouldn't Jimmy Crow cooperate, he turned out to be an accomplished boxer who gave O'Connor a "fierce beating." Why had the newsboy double-crossed him? The answer was a lesson in the endemic deceptiveness of the popular sporting culture of the time. Jimmy Crow wasn't Jimmy Crow. And he wasn't a newsboy. He was Frankie Neil, up-and-coming bantamweight professional boxer. That was a lot of double-crossing for so trivial a purse, but that wasn't all of it. Winnie O'Connor's father had also taken out some insurance, paying Frankie Neil $100 to beat his son. "That was father's idea of humor." Never give a sucker an even (or uneven) break![11]

How much difference did an honest jockey make in winning or losing a race? The first of the thirteen racing maxims of Pittsburgh Phil Smith, the most successful race track bettor of the day, was: "A good jockey, a good horse, a good bet. A poor jockey, a good horse, a moderate bet. A good horse, a moderate jockey, a moderate bet." But how to tell the difference between a good and a moderate jockey? Take the example of two moderate jockeys, Hugh Penny and Aleck Covington, both disciplined for questionable riding. Penny had ridden a "hot favorite" and finished an "indifferent third." Penny's horse subsequently raced twice more, with a different jockey, but didn't do any better. Anyway, Penny's bad riding may have owed more to drink—"he was fond of the cup that cheers as well as inebriates"—than to fraud. Drunkenness in a jockey was not subject to formal penalties. Covington rode badly in finishing third in a race. "He made the plea that he did the best he could, but was cut off two or three times." With a different rider, the same horse, "if possible, performed even worse than when Covington rode her." There was no Jockey Club rule against incompetence. Poor jockeys often rode because trainers and owners had a limited number of alternatives.[12]

Isaac Murphy, the greatest jockey of the
decade before Tod Sloan, admired for
his honesty as well as for his riding skill.

Jockeys considered honest were forgiven much bad riding.
Jockeys with reputations for dishonesty would eventually push
their luck or brazenness too far, even in the loose conditions of
the time. Willie Flynn, who was shameless in his displays of dubious riding, was finally suspended for life. "This verdict met
with hearty approval." Yet there were borderline cases; most cases
seemed to be borderline ones, with the borders being very poorly
defined. Cash Sloan was a poor jockey and a tricky performer
who was suspended numerous times in his career, but he continued to find mounts. Bill Daly was in no doubt about this issue. He gave his boys pragmatic "hard-bitten lectures on honesty": "You can't do crooked work around a track and get away
with it permanently; if you want to get into the big money and
stay there, you have to build a reputation for honesty." Excellent

advice. But many believed that Daly didn't follow it himself. He had a reputation for skirting the rules, or worse. When his horse First Fruit "was so fractious at the post that he threw his jockey," many people assumed that dope had been used, a view a racing writer underlined with heavy irony. "His owner would not, of course, resort to any such expedient, as it is forbidden by the rules." And there were also jockeys known indisputably to be straight, whether they won or lost. At the Bay District track, one day, there was a spontaneous demonstration for Felix Carr. Although he was not a stellar performer, Carr deserved the applause, "a manifestation of public appreciation for an honest jockey's work. No shadow of suspicion of dishonesty hangs over his curly locks." Nevertheless, the greatest ovations were for jockeys who won races, and won money for the bettors cheering them, by whatever means.[13]

Reputation mattered for others as well. When Willie Flynn was suspended, a writer urged the judges to "look further into the matter and find out who was back of Flynn. It is a certainty that he did not take these chances for nothing." Another writer pursued this line of argument about a different case of bad riding. "Who is paying the books for their bad work? When they put up crooked rides someone must pay for it. Someone beside the jockey should be suspended." No doubt. But that wasn't how the world, or at least the horse racing world, actually worked. Trainers were suspended infrequently, and owners very, very rarely. Jockeys were exhorted to report to the stewards when they had a mount that was not in condition to race. But jockeys were not organized as a group; they depended on trainers and owners to give them mounts. And they had their own code of conduct: contempt for anyone who ratted or snitched or blew the whistle.[14]

That came through clearly in the pages of Winnie O'Connor's memoirs, *Jockeys, Crooks and Kings* (1930), a vivid picture of rowdiness, irregularity, and illegality about which no one ever reported a thing. As a very young stable boy O'Connor worked at a number of the better-known outlaw tracks, St. Aspach and Alexander Park, near Washington, D.C. "In my early racing days," O'Connor wrote, "outlawry was not such a novelty." At St. Aspach "they raced about a month under Jockey Club rules, then threw the rules over the fence and adopted banditry," and at Alexander Park, a wild and woolly sports saloon, "anything went but downright murder and all kinds of dope went into horses."

Jockeys picked up ways to fix a race—with the connivance of trainers and stable boys, before the race: feeding a horse just before running (a "filled up" horse can't win); sitting on a horse in its stall all night long, exhausting it; giving a horse the "wobbles" by putting heavy shoes on one front and one back hoof—and without anyone's help, during the race: "a strong but secret pull on the bridle to the right or left, a sway of the body, and the favorite and near favorite are out of the running." O'Connor described how he learned about that classic form of deception, the "ringer," a horse substituted for another horse. One day, as he was working around the stables, a stranger, a trainer of sorts, offered him a chance to exercise his horse, a big bay with a white face and two white forelegs. Soon after, that horse was entered in a race, won, paid a big price, then disappeared. Some time later the stranger reappeared with another horse, also a big bay, but with no markings, and offered O'Connor another job exercising the horse. "The minute I got on him I had the feeling I knew the animal. I suppose every old horseman understands the sixth sense which tells him about a horse. But I kept my mouth shut and rode around." Later O'Connor asked what had become of the other horse. "That's on my farm," the trainer answered, "but this horse is also quiet and you can ride him walking, every morning." After a couple of weeks O'Connor's suspicions became clear to the owner, who responded threateningly: "If you tell anyone, I'll get another boy to ride him mornings and you won't have any horses to ride." "Naturally, I kept my mouth shut."

The bay horse was entered in a race exclusively for horses

that had not previously started at this race meeting. It went off at 30–1 and won easily. "Everybody interested was pleased, and no one else said anything." That night the trainer gave O'Connor a new suit of clothes plus $5 in "real money." The next morning the big bay was gone, and so was his trainer-owner. Soon the newspapers had the whole story. The plain bay was, of course, actually the one with the white face and forelegs, only these had been dyed. "This was the first time I had seen any such 'ringing' as that and I was destined to see a lot more trickery."

What was O'Connor's response to what he had been part of? (His book was written thirty-five years after this incident, but there is no reason to think his views had changed.) "A nine-year-old kid, not long from home, is apt to be tender and sensitive," but such experiences "soon get most of this knocked out of him." And that was a good thing. Such was the unchanging way of the world. Honesty was the best policy when it suited, and when not, not. John Morrissey ran his casino with uncharacteristic honesty because it paid him to do so. "Such were the odds against the players, and such was the number of plungers [at Saratoga] that rich plums fell into his lap without his croupiers furtively shaking the tree." O'Connor endorsed the race track adage "There's no future in wising up suckers. They're born faster than you can get at them." Reform was a middle-class endeavor, and he was contemptuous of it. Late in life he looked back with nostalgia at the "bad old days of open gambling and saloons, when men were men and sometimes tough." He was proud to have mingled with a trio of the most famous outlaw jockeys—Chick Neil, Danny Conroy, and George Wills. "There was nothing about dope racing those boys didn't know."[15]

Along with the venerable forms of cheating, there were newer ways—electricity and dope. At the outlaw tracks the use of electricity was not illegal, and there were many kinds of electrical devices. A battery, held in the palm of the hand, was connected to a finger ring, and when the jockey wanted to give his horse a spurt of energy he pressed the ring against the horse's neck. "That horse instantly went from there." Electric spurs were another innovation. A battery was strapped around the rider's waist, beneath his jacket; a wire ran down each of his legs and connected the battery to the spurs. To get the full effect, both spurs were struck into the horse simultaneously. "The shock made the horse supremely ambitious." Still another device was a small flat battery concealed in the jockey's saddle cloth; by touching a little point on his saddle, the jockey gave the horse "a shock and a burst of speed." Even the whip could be rigged; its handle concealed a small battery from which a fine copper wire ran to a strip of copper near the whip's tip. "When the jockey pressed the button of his battery, and pressed the copper against the horse's flesh, all records were broken for a brief minute."

Less ingenious than electricity, doping was crueler. Dope was usually given in capsule form; the favored ingredients were heroin, strychnine, and digitalis. Sometimes a liquid containing heroin was applied to the horse's skin just in front and in back of the saddle cloth, stinging the horse into frantic motion. Heroin could be put directly on a horse's tongue; or, concealed in a hollow piece of carrot or lump of sugar, it could be given in full view of unsuspecting bystanders. Occasionally liquid dope in a syringe was injected into the left shoulder, near the horse's heart; some horses had a "spot close to the left shoulder that looked like a pin-cushion, it had been jabbed so many times with a needle." Injury was done to horses in less direct ways too. Cocaine and Vaseline were rubbed into horses' legs to deaden pain. Horses with injuries could be made to run but risked permanent injury.

Doping posed difficulties for the dopers. Dope was administered about three-quarters of an hour before a race, so that it would be in full effect when the start came. But long delays at the starting point, a frequent feature of racing in those days, meant that doped horses were often dead on their feet when the start finally came. "Of course, a horse doped regularly became a hop-head, just like a human dope fiend does. He can't do a thing unless he has his dope." None of this bothered the race track crowd, which was without the softer sentiments of middle-class reformers and humanitarians. Bettors cared about doping as a betting matter, not as an ethical one. Winnie O'Connor thought that most bettors were bound to be fooled anyway. "Unless the so-called wise ones are absolutely on the inside how can they know whether a horse they are betting on is doped or not? The answer is, most of them don't know a darned thing about it. Even stable boys aren't always wise." And the effects of doping were unpredictable. One heavily doped horse dropped dead—in the winner's circle.

Most benign tricks drew on new technology. At Electric Light Park, St. Louis, night racing was introduced in 1892–93 and quickly spread to other places—Savannah, Georgia; Covington, Kentucky; Algiers, near New Orleans; two Boston tracks; and the Maspeth track on Long Island, which offered five afternoon races and five more beginning at 8 P.M. Searchlights followed the horses around the track. The lighting was erratic. There were dark spots; strange things happened in those dark places. "'Twas a great game for trustful sporting gentlemen."[16]

The darkest place of all, during a race, is what is in the jockey's mind and how this is unmistakably communicated to the horse. The pervasive ambiguity of horse racing, in this particular relationship, is ultimately impenetrable. Neither the trustful nor the untrustful can know for sure. Many a bettor and observer has thought, "If only horses could talk." The folk wisdom of the turf about this was summed up in words attributed to the English sports writer R. S. Surtees: "There is no secret so close as that between a rider and his horse."

This was the horse racing culture Tod Sloan inherited and accepted unquestioningly when he began riding in California.

# C A L I F O R N I A

orses raced in California for decades before Tod Sloan got there. Travelers in the 1820s and 1830s were struck by the fondness of the Spanish Californians for the sport. In 1835, Richard Henry Dana identified race courses in San Francisco, Los Angeles, on the beach at Santa Barbara, and along the banks of the San Diego River. And then, with the Mexican War, the coming of the Yankees, the Gold Rush, and California statehood, all this was wiped out. But in the new American settlements the old forms were re-created. The Pioneer Course, the first California race track built on the English model, opened in 1851, operating under the rules of the Union Jockey Club of New York. It was followed by the Pavilion and the Union tracks, and by many others. "No fewer than eight race courses are buried beneath the streets of present day San Francisco."[1]

Racing was only one manifestation of the speculative mania that touched all aspects of Gold Rush California. The owners and developers of the new tracks were speculators who had made fortunes and managed to keep them. These men subsequently dominated California business and politics, transforming themselves into models of social respectability. In 1863, Senator George Hearst was a leader in the construction of the Bay View track. In 1874, Governor Leland Stanford was associated with the building of the Bay District track. Tanforan, a track that proved to be longer lived than any of its contemporaries, opened in 1889; its sponsors, exotic as well as respectable, were an English nobleman, Lord Talbot Clifton, and a Polish prince, Andre Poniatowski, with financial backing from the unexotic but very rich William Crocker. In 1895, Adolph Spreckels, a sugar heir, and others organized the Pacific Coast Jockey Club and founded the Ingleside track. In the years when Tod Sloan was racing in California there were scheduled race meetings at more than forty towns and cities.

The California horseman most representative of the popular culture of the time was Elias Jackson "Lucky" Baldwin (1828–1909). Born and raised on farms in Ohio and Indiana, he grew up in Sloan-like circumstances, poorly educated and living by his wits. A shrewd horse bargainer, Baldwin won $200 racing a horse of his own; he used that money to open a saloon and a hotel in Indiana. In 1853 he gave that up and went to the speculator's paradise, California. There he made a killing buying and selling mineral claims and other real estate, eventually investing heavily in theaters, hotels, and horses.

A number of things separated Lucky Baldwin from his nabob contemporaries. He traveled to India and Japan and brought back a Japanese theatrical troupe that he promoted in New York City. He avidly courted personal publicity and created an identifiable personal style, marked by a wide black hat and a long black coat, a kind of small, solemn-faced, stingy-looking version of Mark Twain. Baldwin was completely open in his pursuit of money and women. "The rest of the world could go

Lucky Baldwin epitomized the spirit of California racing in Tod Sloan's day. "His character, for better or worse, was his own. The rest of the world could go hang. He would do as he pleased, and he did" (Glasscock, *Lucky Baldwin*). Arboretum of Los Angeles County, Historical Section.

hang. He would do as he pleased, and he did. If he was a sinner, he would be a glorious sinner. He was no hypocrite." Even in wide-open San Francisco in the 1890s the sexual affairs of the notables were carefully concealed. "The names of California millionaires whose power extended across the continent were protected." Insiders knew about the wild parties on the notorious upper floor of the respectable Occidental Hotel and what went on in certain suites in the equally respectable Russ House, but the general public did not. Baldwin, who married three times, ignored subterfuge and as a result was thought by proper society to be depraved. Nor did he pretend to any pangs of religious conscience. He was a "professing disciple of Robert Ingersoll"—the notorious atheist of the day—and a "practicing disciple of Casanova." Pretty women pursued him as he pursued them, and, when necessary, "to some, under pressure, he gave thousands of dollars."

Baldwin and Sloan. Lucky Baldwin's racing colors, a black-and-red Maltese cross, were a familiar sight on tracks across the country for a number of years; his horses won three American Derbies at Washington Park, Chicago. But it doesn't appear that Tod Sloan ever rode for him. Anyway, Baldwin's importance in the history of American racing wasn't connected with San Francisco. He came into the possession of an immense and spectacularly beautiful tract of land in southern California, which he called Rancho Santa Anita, the site of a race track he built in 1904. It became one of the major American race tracks of the twentieth century. The connection between Baldwin and Sloan was probably not conscious imitation on Sloan's part, but a deeper matter: the absorption by him of Baldwin's values: "aggressiveness, individual independence, defiance of restrictions and scorn of convention."[2]

San Francisco was the center of California racing, and the leading racing establishment of the 1890s was the Bay District track, just north of the western end of Golden Gate Park. Betting was heavy: "a vast amount of gold was flying around the bet-ting ring." The racing season was astoundingly long—from No-vember to the following June, more than two hundred days of racing. Gambling fever had hit California again, "like measles in a tenement district." Observers were blunt about the pervasive corruption—"the racing at Bay District is very bad . . . an un-derhand game has been in progress for some time"—and matter of fact in noting the occasional exceptions to the prevailing spirit of things, as with the example of a jockey named Spence, "one of the few honest jockeys riding on the coast," or of an owner like Lucky Baldwin, of whom a sports editor wrote: "I never knew but one good thing about him: he never threw a race." Turfmen and gamblers were increasingly coming to San Francisco for winter racing, leaving behind New Orleans. "The game is a little tame in that city." There were no illusions about what brought many to the track. "Horse racing without betting these days is out of the question. They would not draw a little bit." Certainly, Bay District and the track that supplanted it, Ingleside, drew well, with crowds of as many as eight thousand. Women came in large numbers—Thursday was Ladies' Day. Audiences were noisy and raucous. After one especially unpop-ular decision, "the crowd surged about the judges' enclosure in a menacing way with yells, catcalls and wild gestures."[3]

In the circumstances, the California Jockey Club did well to keep a semblance of order. Stewards conducted investigations; jockeys, trainers, and owners were reprimanded, fined, and sus-pended; but still things went on that were best not inquired too closely into. "If the horses which contested the last race could talk, their stories would probably make interesting reading . . . but bets were paid accordingly." Many stables were owned by bookmakers, including George Rose. Tod Sloan would ride for him. What choice, really, did jockeys have? Rose, often involved in shady dealings, had been "warned off"—banished—from Bay District, then reinstated. In one race Sloan rode Rose's Gilead, a big favorite, and finished second. "With any kind of

The backstretch at Bay District Race Track, San Francisco,
in the 1890s. California Historical Society, Luke Fay Collection,
FN-19547.

strong ride, Gilead would have won easily." The crowd was infuriated, but it was common knowledge that Rose's bookmakers
were betting against Gilead. There were many such happenings.
And yet the writer for a local newspaper, who had candidly detailed many of them, had also, in fairness, to write, "Because bettors and bookmakers are suspicious of George Rose, it does not
follow that he is guilty. Why do not his accusers come to the stewards with evidence?" There were numerous scandals, but not all
involved illegality. Wildwood, a very heavy favorite, finished out
of the money. He wasn't "pulled" by his jockey; "he was in no
condition to race." His owner didn't want him to run but had
"leased" him to someone who did run him, "as many have cause
to regret."[4]

Gambling wasn't the only problem. Drugs were copiously,
openly, and legally administered, as a brief description of the terrible White Cloud incident makes clear. "The owner of the
chestnut gelding White Cloud had it in his mind to make a
killing yesterday, and he succeeded, but it was the horse that was

killed instead of the ring of bookmakers. White Cloud came out in a field of lizards in the last race and was backed down from 4–1 to 2–1. When he went to the post his eyeballs were distended to twice their normal size and he displayed other unmistakable signs of having a strong 'jolt' in him. He was fairly rabid at the post, and ran away with [his jockey], making the circuit of the track twice. When he reached the post on the second lap, he dropped dead."

As at all of the respectable tracks, bookmakers were tolerated because they brought in much money to the track. The Bay District made available every facility for losing money—nineteen or more regular bookmakers, a field book, three combination books, one pari-mutuel box, and a wheel of fortune; it received more than $2,000 a day in fees from them. At the Oakland track, which operated in defiance of the San Francisco Jockey Club, there were wheels of fortune, chuck-a-luck, and dice games, if racing wasn't enough. And the big bettors of the day were not just tolerated but much admired. The great figure at Bay District was Riley Grannan, a flamboyant westerner in his twenties who was known for the size of his bets—rivaling those of Bet-a-Million-Gates—and the insouciance with which he won and lost. In 1896, in one day, Grannan "scorched the ring," winning $20,000; despite that, it was said, he was "still behind the game this season." There is a verbal portrait of him in action.

> "Here's 55 to 100, Captain Rees, come and get it."
> "I'll bet you $1,000."
> "You're on."[5]

In spite of his insistence on his own incompetence as a rider, by the winter of 1894 Tod had already established something of a reputation; early accounts describe him as having "many friends" in the Bay Area, and he was included among the "many celebrities of the pig skin," one of the slang terms for jockey. Nevertheless, his early riding efforts were fumbling ones. In the first two weeks of January, he finished third ("show," in racing lingo), sixth, third, and eleventh in one week, and twelfth, third, fifth, and last in the next. In between, on January 4, he won a race; the newspaper writer's comments and misspelling of his name make clear his neophyte status: "Sloane let go Francesca's head turning into the straight and Francesca finished in front, something out of the expected."[6]

On January 12, Tod had a close call. Riding Ed Stanley, he and the horse fell on the first turn; it seemed the horse had fallen on Tod, but he somehow escaped injury, though the horse had to be destroyed. The racing correspondent's laconic report was surprising: "Ed Stanley had only recently been purchased by Sloan for $1,200, so the young rider's loss is quite a heavy one." Where did Tod Sloan get the money? We'll never know. But the accident reminded anyone who needed reminding that death or serious injury was an immediate but unmentionable possibility for a jockey every time he rode. "It happens, it happens. There's nothing to talk about," Tod said. The greatest jockeys have been the ones most willing to take a chance at a crucial moment, and this may be connected with the recklessness of their lives off the track.[7]

Throughout the winter there was little change in the pattern of Sloan's performance—usually unplaced, occasionally in the money, a victory now and then. The few comments about his riding were usually favorable, however: "came up at the finish very fast under the vigorous riding of Sloan"; and "Sloan nursed Malcolm along and coming fast at the end won cleverly." He was riding enough for another aspect of his work to begin to come into prominence: his riding was suspiciously erratic. On the favorite San Luis Rey, Sloan finished second. "A peculiar race; the horse did nothing, strange to relate." But when he finished sixth on Tigress he "caused a whole lot of comment." The reporter didn't mince his words. "[Tigress] was well backed by the general public and it certainly looked as if Sloan gave them the double cross. At all events, the stewards have suspended the jockey pending an investigation. The book makers as well as the jockey should be made to pay, if anything is discovered." Nothing was discovered. Tod continued to ride after his suspension was lifted.[8]

Again and again one confronts the essential ambiguity of the sport; it was always difficult and often impossible to distinguish between riding that was incompetent, riding that was careless, and riding that was intentionally bad. When Tod rode a favorite and finished second, "beaten decisively," there were no questions; his horse should never have been favored. But when he finished third with Trix, a horse he had had success with, "it looked as if Sloan kept Trix back until it was too late." Looked—to whom? Was this anything other than the faulty judgment of an inexperienced rider? A jockey rode against his rivals but he also rode against the bettor's expectations. Even so, Sloan revealed a predilection for getting into scrapes. He rode Royal Flush to a dead heat for first but his horse was disqualified when Tod weighed in two pounds under his assigned weight. Tod insisted that the explanation was that he had weighed in and out on different scales. A writer suggested that he was not guilty, but on interesting grounds. "He is altogether too shrewd to take any chances by slipping only two pounds. If Sloan had weighed in five or six pounds short, it would have been natural to suspect that some 'funny business' had been attempted." And this writer noted that Tod was rapidly losing popularity because of such repeated incidents.[9] We are a long way here from innocence.

In 1895, again at the Bay District track, Tod Sloan came into his own, and the fickle racing public made him a hero. He started slowly again, winning only occasionally in January and February. And then in March and April and May he burst forth brilliantly. He won five races in two days. "The midget man is riding in great form." And in a new style: "Boreas got well away and gave Tod Sloan an opportunity to assume his prettiest seat while galloping up the stretch." Fast starts and blazing finishes. His sense of pace was improving dramatically. He began to win races in bunches—two one day, then three a few days later, "putting up great races," winning on Gold Bug, a 30–1 long shot, in a five-horse finish "that was the best ever seen at the Bay District track."[10]

Tod's reputation rose with trainers and owners, as well as with the general public. He was now in great demand. The famous lawman Wyatt Earp had a small stable, and Tod rode his colors, navy blue polka dots on a white field, to victory twice in one day. "Our stable was, of course, much too small to keep on the payroll such a highly paid jockey," Earp's wife wrote; he was lent to them as a favor by one of the bigger stables.[11] One time he was given a retainer *not* to ride. And he was developing his reputation as a character, a bumptious and cocky lightweight, his youth and smallness giving him a special kind of charm. "It is amusing to see Tod playing marbles [with the other jockeys] and smoking a cigar a foot long in the paddock between races." Bobbing and driving down the stretch, crouching forward with a kind of intense fury, there is a kaleidoscope of images: a "star-shooting drive," "covered himself with glory," "came on with the speed of a cloud burst," "looking over his shoulder at the girls in the stands." This boy-man, trickster-innocent, "receiving a round of applause."

"SLOAN IN GREAT FORM" was a headline now, whereas three months before he was barely mentioned by name. "Tod Sloan, the midget man, is making the record of his life." "If he escapes a swelling of the cranium, he has a chance to earn enough money this summer to place himself on the sunny side of easy street for the remainder of his life." Tod Sloan on easy street! "His riding of Empress of Norfolk and Rear Guard yesterday was so high class that he really deserves special mention." Had it not been for his jockeyship, "coming down the stretch like an Iowa cyclone," the sulking Rear Guard "could have been defeated just as easily as he won." Now the triumphs came day after day: "Sloan rode two sensational finishes," "Sloan electrified the crowd," the Lilliputian celebrating with one of his huge cigars that looked as big as a broom handle.[12]

Measuring Tod Sloan's success in California by counting his winners is misleading because he rode fewer times than other leading jockeys. He was selective in his mounts, at times capricious, often tactlessly making clear his lack of interest in horses offered to him. Nor was he regular in his training habits. He often diverted himself until the early hours and was not eager, to say the least, for morning workouts. This willful attitude amused some, infuriated others. The measure of success that mattered most to him was his winning percentage. In 1895 that was 28 percent—he won 57 times in 205 attempts. In 1896, a year in which the jockey with the largest number of winners had a winning percentage of 20 percent, Tod had 68 winners out of 219 mounts, a sensational 31 percent average. No wonder he quickly became a favorite with the betting public.

Such success was a good deal for a rider to have achieved in so short a time, but there was also a different measure of success, a chain of events that would eventually have international consequences, nothing less than the revolutionizing of the art of riding.

# SIX

# FORWARD SEAT

What did Tod Sloan do to convert a mediocre career into a stellar one? He adopted a new style of riding, the "forward seat," or "forward crouch." As he recalled it years later, what he did and how he did it merged into one dramatic moment. One day he and another jockey were galloping their horses together when his horse started to bolt; in trying to regain control Tod climbed up out of the saddle and onto the horse's neck. His fellow jockey laughed at the strange sight, and "I laughed louder than he." On reflection Tod realized that "when I was doing that neck crouch, the horse's stride seemed to be freer and that it was easier for me too."

> I put two and two together and thought there must be something in it, and I began to think it out, trying all sorts of experiments on horses at home. The

"crouch seat," or the "monkey mount," or the thousand and one other ways it has been described, was the result. Then the time came when I determined to put it into practice. But I couldn't screw up enough courage the first time I had a chance. I kept putting it off. At last, though, I did really spring it on them. Everybody laughed. They thought I had turned comedian. But I was too cocksure to be discouraged. I was certain that I was on the right track. I persevered, and at last I began to win races![1]

The forward crouch was a remarkably simple innovation. The jockey, with short stirrups and short reins, moved up until he was high on the horse's withers, the highest part of the back, between the shoulder blades, leaning forward on the neck of the horse, looking down over its head. It is how all jockeys ride today and have done for a century. It is as difficult for us to imagine another way of riding as it was for many of Tod's contemporaries to imagine any alternative to what they had known. For two hundred years jockeys had ridden far back in the saddle, uprightly perpendicular to the horse, using long stirrups and long reins, the rider a point of calm stability as the horse stretched its legs out ahead and behind. This languidly elegant classic style is what we see in work by generations of painters, from eighteenth-century depictors of English racing, such as George Stubbs and Richard Roper, to the nineteenth-century Frenchmen Théodore Géricault and Edgar Degas. This was not simply the classic style of riding. It was the *only* style. Apparently it had not occurred to anyone to imagine an alternative; and even after someone had, tradition's power was so great that intelligent observers refused to accept its overthrow. In the heartfelt words of a contemporary English observer, "It may be insular, narrow-minded, prejudiced, and the rest of it, but I cannot believe that, generation after generation, jockeys have been sitting on the wrong part of a horse's back, that the best place for the saddle is not where it has

An 1870s print of the horse Harry Bassett defeating Longfellow in a
match race at Saratoga. The jockeys are riding in the conventional, Old
World style. Currier and Ives print, National Museum of Racing,
Saratoga Springs, New York.

always been, and that at the end of the nineteenth century the
theory and practice of horsemanship as applied to racing is to be
revolutionised."[2]

Yet that is what happened. Tod Sloan apparently imagined
an alternative to the classic style, realized it in practice, and revolutionized riding. Even the word "revolutionized" is inadequate
for what happened. Few revolutions have been this complete.
Within half a dozen years the old style was obliterated. Despite
the bitter opposition to the new style, many racing people
quickly took in its practical advantages. It significantly reduced
wind resistance. It moved the rider's center of gravity forward
and afforded him a better look ahead. It gave a jockey, especially
a lightweight jockey, greater control over his mount.

The disadvantages boiled down to fear that the forward
seat put too much weight on the forelegs of the horse and in-

creased the likelihood of breakdowns. This turned out not to be the case. Actually, much of the opposition was aesthetic. The crouching figure, bobbing about on the neck of the horse, was unpleasing to look at. Traditionalists hated the "hammer and tongs" style, maintaining that "in the old days a race was a far prettier thing to watch." You cannot oppose it, but you cannot like it," one horseman said, expressing the views of many. "It has spoilt much of the beauty of race riding, but it has come to stay, and we must make the best of it."[3]

The full story of what Tod Sloan did, however, is more complex than his own account suggests. His description of his moment of inspiration and of his determination to "spring" the new style on an unsuspecting racing world makes dramatic reading. It is also misleading. One of the puzzling aspects of the story of the forward seat is that contemporary California racing accounts seem to have failed to mention it. If a startling novelty was introduced, shattering the spell of the past, racing writers failed to notice it. They didn't use the term "forward seat" or "forward crouch," didn't describe it as the "monkey crouch," didn't mock Tod Sloan for the way he rode. Observers noted his rapidly growing success but didn't connect it with an epoch-making innovation.

How could this be? Part of the explanation has to do with the difficulties we face in knowing the ordinary past. Much of the racing past we would like to know is unreclaimable; the story of something as common and trivial as this got little attention. Procedures and customs such as these were customary, taken for granted, needing and receiving little comment. Reporting was, at most, partial and rudimentary. Tod Sloan's own recollection of the past was obviously self-interested; he didn't pretend to be a neutral observer or even to think in those terms. Twenty years later he recalled the past as we all recall it, partially, obscurely— or sometimes the reverse of this, with a misleading clarity. Perhaps, as well, when the forward seat had become the famous monkey seat and he was dictating his memoirs, he realized that his story required a heroic moment appropriate to it. Or perhaps there was such a moment as he described when, galloping a horse in a warm-up, his mastery of himself as a rider and of the horse he was riding came powerfully together, a moment when in a rush of self-awareness he realized the possibilities of the forward seat. That doesn't contradict the main thing we must keep in mind: that Tod Sloan's new racing style, and that of his contemporaries, revealed itself gradually, as a continuous evolution, not as a single moment.

To add to the ambiguity, Tod insisted that he never rode in an actual "forward" seat—that is, with very short reins and stirrups—but only in a *somewhat* forward position. "It was a very false idea that I rode short; that was left to those who followed me." Whatever the origins of the new position, Tod was very clear about what happened once it had come into being as an identifiable style: other jockeys copied it and pushed it to extremes. Cash Sloan agreed with this view, and he was in a good position to know. "Tod's [style] is perhaps a little exaggerated, but I ride forward, and I ride shorter than Tod."[4] And in any event, Tod's way of riding was not one fixed and final thing. He adapted it to different conditions, different places. His style was only one of the skills that vaulted him into a position of supremacy among his peers.

Where did the forward seat come from? Tod gave some credit to Harry Griffin, the jockey among his contemporaries whom he most admired. "He was far and away the greatest." Tod had seen Griffin "with short stirrups and leaning over the horse." But if Griffin's riding suggested the forward seat to Tod, Griffin was never publicly identified with it by anyone else, never claimed it as his own. A common explanation was asserted by writers and observers at the time: Tod picked up hints of it from the white and African-American stable boys who exercised horses without proper equipment and with no previous training; and there was the still older tradition of Native Americans riding bareback up on the necks of their horses.

A variant of this, both culturally broader and geographically more specific, was proposed by J. Huggins, a prominent American trainer of the time, who believed that this kind of riding came from the "up country" race meetings at small rural tracks. Always on the lookout for talent, Huggins went from one country meeting to another, taking along an ordinary horse from his stable, which he used as a yardstick for measuring performance. If a "country" horse beat his horse, Huggins bought the country horse and took it home, assuming that good training would further improve its performance. But he was surprised to find that this often did not happen; the country horse would be beaten by the Huggins horse it had defeated on its home turf. And this occurred too frequently to be explained by chance.

One day Huggins stumbled on an explanation. He bought a country horse that had been ridden by an African-American stable boy who begged to be taken along with the horse. Huggins agreed, but when they got back to his stable, it was the same old story: the horse ran badly. The stable boy said to him, "You let me ride and you will see what will happen." Sure enough. "The horse and the black boy rolled home." *It was the riders who made the difference,* riders who, not having learned the old style, rode in the new one. "They rode as they could," Huggins recounted. "Often they rode with only a rug instead of a saddle, and they used to catch hold of the mane and hang on the best way they could until they found their balance."[5] The evolution of this indigenous American racing style was in every sense a grass-roots movement, drawing on white riders and African Americans, on stable boys and beginners, all of them untrained in the traditional way. It was in the country, after all, that the most distinctive aspect of American racing began: dirt race tracks supplanting turf courses. The American style grew up side by side with the traditional upright style that dominated at the larger tracks, especially in the East.

The comments of an English traveler in the 1870s, making allowances for the exaggerated language, bring this common

Horses passing the finish stand at Saratoga in the 1880s, with the jockeys
riding in a somewhat more forward seat. Note that the artist has
portrayed the horses running with all four feet off the ground, a much-
disputed capability until photography proved that it was possible.

style vividly to life. He described "a black boy [who had] got his
saddle forward on his horse's withers, his feet apparently kicking at his horse's mouth." This method was not limited just to
African Americans. "It would be difficult to say which ride
worse, the white or black boys, so bad are both." The traveler's
disgust over what he had seen was the same as that provoked by
Tod Sloan's riding twenty years later. Especially revealing is his

bafflement that this style of riding worked so well. "The extraordinary part of the business is," he exclaimed, "that such great speed should be attained with such wretched jockey-ship."[6]

African Americans played an important role in the history of both styles of American riding. Before the Civil War many featherweight jockeys were slaves. Some slave owners were alleged to have bred slaves for small size, others to have kept small boys on a starvation diet to prevent their growing too large. Whatever their age they were called "boys" and were known by their first names—"Abe," "Washington," "Cato." After the Civil War they were not limited to jobs as stable boys or to the small tracks. They rode at all the major tracks. Abe Hawkins, said to have been a former slave from Louisiana, was one of the leading riders in the country in the 1860s. He won the inaugural race at Jerome Park in 1866, and another African-American jockey won the inaugural race at Saratoga.

The Kentucky Derby, at Louisville's Churchill Downs track, was dominated by African-American riders for its first quarter-century, from Oliver Lewis, who won the first Derby aboard Aristides in 1876, through William Walker, Erskine Henderson, George Lewis, Babe Hurd, Isaac Lewis, Alonzo Clayton, James Perkins, Willie Simms, and James Winkfield. Simms and Winkfield won two Derbies apiece, Simms in 1896 and 1898, Winkfield in 1901 and 1902. Of the first twenty-eight Kentucky Derbies, fifteen winning mounts were ridden by eleven different African Americans. In the 1880s and 1890s African-American jockeys won the American Derby at Washington Park in Chicago, Pimlico's Preakness, and the Belmont Stakes.

The lithographs and drawings of the time reveal that African-American jockeys employed a number of riding styles, from the traditional English way to the emerging American forward style, a contrast exemplified by the differing styles of Isaac Murphy and Willie Simms. Murphy (1861–96), the preeminent African-American rider of the era and one of the greatest

American riders of any time, began riding at fourteen; soft spoken, gentle in manner, he was much admired and loved. He won the Kentucky Derby in 1884, 1890, and 1891. Of the 1,412 mounts in his riding career Murphy won on 628, an astounding lifetime winning percentage of 44 percent. "Murphy is the only jockey in the entire history of the turf who would have shown a profit for gamblers who made a flat bet on every horse he rode." There was never any suggestion that Murphy's riding style was exaggerated; the easy mastery and purity of his form were what observers noted. "He sat straight as an arrow in his saddle." Another description of him was on the great horse Salvator: "imperturbable, sitting well down in his saddle and straight as a dart," the classical picture of proper form, "the idealization of horse and rider."[7]

The successor to Murphy among African-American jockeys was Willie Simms, one of the leading riders in the mid-1890s. He won two Belmonts in 1893 and 1894, as well as his two Kentucky Derbies and the Preakness. In 1894, when Tod Sloan was struggling to establish himself in California, Simms was enjoying spectacular success at the best tracks in the East, with 228 victories out of 688 mounts. In America, Simms was not identified as riding unusually forward, but in 1895, when he made an abbreviated appearance in England, his style, anticipating the response to Tod Sloan there, was thought bizarre. In an interview in 1900 when his career was almost at its end, the modest Simms looked back at the way the forward seat had taken over on American race tracks and proudly and accurately asserted his place in that development. "I claim to be one of the first boys to adopt the forward seat and I ride with practically the same seat now that I did when I was on top of the heap in this country." With equal pride he insisted that his success was based on more than simply a style of riding. "For myself, I am not so sure that the forward seat has so very much to do with [success]."[8]

Of course some people refused to accept the idea that this revolutionary development resulted from an evolutionary collective process. In a culture prizing individualism, the search was always to identify the one autonomous inventor. A few years after the forward seat had become identified as a style in itself associated with Tod Sloan, a writer argued that an owner and trainer named Frank Van Ness should be credited with its invention, if not with its implementation. In this version of the story, Van Ness supposedly taught the style to Tod. Van Ness met Sloan in Chicago, recognized that he was not riding well, took him to California, and spent a great deal of time teaching him "how to hold his hands and cling to a horse with his knees." Tod's old habits were hard to shake. "Tossed on the back of a horse he would start, but soon drop into loose methods." Van Ness placed himself, it was said, at different points around the track and threw clods of dirt at Tod to help him stick to the new style.[9]

Van Ness and Sloan were in San Francisco at the same time over a two-year period, the period of Sloan's rise to prominence. And Sloan rode a number of horses for Van Ness's stable. Who knows? Perhaps Van Ness did contribute something to Sloan's technique as a rider. However, the description of Tod's riding style is vague, and Van Ness, in his own right, never claimed that the idea was his. It may well be that Sloan learned other things from Van Ness, things that did him no good at all. "The horses from the Van Ness stable have a system of their own," a racing correspondent reported. "When a Van Ness horse looks to have a moral certainty, he generally finishes last. When he looks to have no chance, he often comes in first." As another writer said, in another connection: "These 'natural inconsistencies' are an interesting study. The place to study them is in the betting ring."[10]

This is the first half of the story of the forward seat. Tod Sloan's stylistic innovation hadn't merited much attention except occasionally to be identified as crude, at the "cowboy" end of the spectrum. Observers sometimes rebuked what they perceived as slovenliness. When an African-American jockey named Clay, riding in "admirable style," defeated Tod in a race, a newspaper writer thought it fair that the "comic opera jockey Sloan had to play second fiddle."[11] He didn't play second fiddle often, however, or for long. Ridicule never stopped him. Wherever he got his ideas, people recognized Sloan's persistence—audacity, even—in pushing on in his own way, appreciated that he had an overall conception of how a race should be run. Then other American jockeys seized on what he had begun, pushed it further, swept everything else away.

Winning made the difference. The forward seat would have come to nothing if it hadn't won races. And chance played a role. If Willie Simms had succeeded in England in 1895 it might well have been he who was identified with the forward seat; but it was Tod Sloan whose fame spread to every quarter of the thoroughbred racing world. And once Sloan became synonymous with the new style, most people didn't bother about distinctions between popularizing and inventing. That was the result of the second chapter of the Tod Sloan story. If the evolution of the forward seat was American, its notoriety as the monkey seat was English; and this not only fixed Sloan's fame, it also shaped the way people looked at the beginning of the American story. The climax of that story lies ahead, across the Atlantic.

Tod Sloan was familiar with another innovation in American horse racing in these years, the starting gate.

In the traditional method of starting, jockeys walked their horses toward the starting post under the supervision (control would be too strong a term) of two starters. The starter at the post dropped a flag when he believed that the horses were more or less equally ready to run; however, if the start proved to be very uneven, the second man, farther down the track, also dropped his flag, and the horses returned for another attempt. The same method pertained if the horses, instead of walking up to the starting post, came to a full stop there, awaiting the drop of the first flag.

Starts under this system were the most unsatisfactory aspect of racing; they were often wildly unfair. Many horses were left at the post, losing dozens of yards to their opponents. False starts were equally frustrating and exhausting for horses and jockeys. And no part of racing was more tiresome and unsatisfactory for the spectators. Delays at the post of fifteen or twenty minutes were common and expected; longer delays were frequent, with horses and jockeys sometimes waiting forty-five minutes or more. The record for frustration and futility at the starting post was perhaps the American Derby at Washington Park in 1893, when there were twenty-five false starts; it took two hours to get the field off. Starting was as hotly debated as finishing. Starters varied greatly in their coolness and in their judgment; jockeys and starters often engaged in furious verbal exchanges, or worse; some starters equipped themselves with whips and lashed jockeys for disobedience. At the St. Louis race track, in 1892, a starter was shot. Long delays at the post made orderly scheduling of races difficult, and it was almost impossible to have more than five races in an afternoon.

The starting gate was originated in Australia in the 1880s and brought to the western United States in the early 1890s. There were numerous versions of it, as racing people alternately resisted it and tried to improve it. The early starting gate wasn't a gate at all; it essentially consisted of a band of webbing stretched across the track at the starting post. The horses stood before this until the starter thought they formed an orderly and even line, at which point the webbing was raised and the horses sent off. There were difficulties with this type of gate, as horses bunched up in front of it and there was danger of entanglement. But the same was true of the traditional way of starting. Trainers could (and eventually did) train their horses in the use of the gate; but many were lazy and obdurately opposed its use.

Nevertheless, the starting gate moved east for trials, and it was introduced in England in 1897 and more rapidly accepted there than in the United States. The Bay District track experimented with it in 1896, which gave Tod valuable experience for when he encountered it in the East and in England. The long delays at the post hadn't, in a sense, mattered much in the old style of distance racing, because a few dozen yards didn't count for much and the pace was slower. But with shorter races and with speed at a premium, an improved version of starting was essential.

Tod had done what he could do in California and had learned, for better and worse, what he was to learn about racing life. California and California racing had much to commend it, and he would return to it; but to reach the next rung on the ladder of success he had to compete against the best horses and riders. And that meant eastern racing. So he headed for New York.

# SEVEN

# GAY NINETIES

Bty the mid-1890s, when Tod Sloan got to New York, the spectacular growth of horse racing as a spectator sport in the United States had resulted in more than three hundred race tracks, large and small, legitimate and outlaw. Nowhere had expansion been so dramatic as in and around New York City, where there were six race tracks in operation, each with its own character and clientele, competing against one another for patronage, rising and falling in popularity. No sooner was something established as traditional than it was replaced by something else, something new.

Jerome Park was by this time only a memory, gobbled up by land-hungry New York City. Monmouth Park, located at Long Branch, New Jersey, then a fashionable resort, was the most venerable of Jerome Park's successors. Catering to the political and theatrical crowd, it had been rebuilt in the late 1870s and then again in 1890, emerging as the biggest racing plant in America. It covered six hundred acres, the track was a mile and three-quarters around, and the grandstand, entirely of iron, was seven hundred feet long. It had the longest meeting of any of the New York tracks, July and August, and the racing was clockwise, European style.

Leonard Jerome had continued to play a major role in New York racing through the 1880s. He and others formed the Coney Island Jockey Club and, in 1880, opened a track at Sheepshead Bay, Long Island. Its charming seaside atmosphere caught the popular fancy; so did its mix of ordinary folks with the socially conscious, and with the "youth and beauty of the New York stage." Its most notable race was the Futurity, which, by the 1890s, offered a fabulous purse—$68,000. Jerome also had had a hand in creating Morris Park, the most elegant race track of this period, the one that aspired to appeal to the New York social elite. It was built on a 330-acre site in Westchester County, with a palatial clubhouse and excellent facilities. It inherited several of Jerome Park's most prestigious races—the Belmont Stakes, the Withers, and the Champagne Stakes—and added a new one, the Metropolitan Handicap.

There were three race tracks in the area designed to appeal to the masses. Brighton Beach was a model business operation, unpretentious and efficient. Betting was always heavy there. A newspaper article of 1894 gives an idea of the scale of wagering: sixty bookmakers on average, handling an average of $3,000 per race per day; the gross, for a typical afternoon, was more than $1 million. Gravesend, in Flatbush, Brooklyn, opened in 1886 and was operated by Michael and Philip Dwyer, Brooklyn natives. Like its proprietors, Gravesend was determinedly proletarian in style, a low-maintenance operation. Racing was on Mondays, Wednesdays, and Fridays, alternating with Sheepshead Bay's Tuesdays, Thursdays, and Saturdays. Gravesend had one popular major race, the Brooklyn Handicap, first run in 1887. Aqueduct, established by the Queens County Jockey Club, was a result of the desire to emulate the financial success of Brighton

The track at Sheepshead Bay, New York. Its charming seaside atmosphere caught the popular fancy and attracted ordinary folks, the socially conscious, and the theatrical racing crowd. Keeneland Library.

Beach and Gravesend. There, too, economy and social unpretentiousness were the overriding concerns. Its clubhouse was derided as a "shanty held up by stilts," but large crowds came anyway, and eventually the plant was remodeled and made more attractive. Its greatest days lay ahead, in the next century.[1]

Legal gambling was probably the chief reason that more and more of the huge urban population went to the nearby tracks. But it was part of a larger phenomenon. Entertainment was a hallmark of the 1890s, and one reason why—despite financial panic and protracted depression, racial segregation and lynchlaw, furious political acrimony and imperialist expansion—the decade came to be known as the Gay Nineties. What made the decade gay was the perceptible easing of social and moral restraints. Traditional sobriety and restraint were challenged by playfulness and ease: "easy come, easy go, easy honor, easy morals."[2]

Sporting and theatrical cultures were intertwined. Racing

and theatrical people had much in common: both had been disdained by respectable people; both represented partial escape from puritanical conventions. "Racing went along with the Gay Nineties up to the hilt," one observer noted. And so did the theater. In 1896, Florenz Ziegfeld, until then notable only as manager of Sandow the Strong Man, produced a musical play, *The Parlor Match,* in which the alluring Anna Held sang a song that posed a provocative question—"Won't You Come and Play With Me?"

> I have such a nice little way with me,
>     A way with me,
>     A way with me,
> I have such a nice little way with me
> I should like to have you play with me,
> Play with me all the day long.[3]

Play. Race tracks and theaters were notoriously synonymous with play, horseplay, playing around, foolish idleness.

Sporting theatrical culture was flash. And the man who personified the flashy style, ostentatious show, and shameless self-indulgence was the man known to his parents as James Buchanan Brady but to everyone else as Diamond Jim. He rejoiced in his "illuminated shirt-front," complete sets of shirt studs, cuff and waistcoat buttons, one of diamonds, others of sapphires, rubies, and amethysts, a different display every night of the month, "winks and ripples of light sparking like a thousand mirrors." Diamond Jim craved notoriety. "You fellers can talk all you like about what's done and what ain't," he said to reporters. "As for me, I've always noticed that them as has 'em wears 'em." The lines between work and play were blurring. Wall Street was flash, too. Not diamonds, stocks. Fabulous amounts of money were won in the greatest casino of all, its patrons the "swaggering, blustering men whose fortunes were being made exploiting and developing the continent and its resources and who were eager to play."[4]

The center of theatrical and sporting life in these years was Harry Hill's, a cluster of buildings that combined a theater, a restaurant, and a bar. In a prize ring set up on the theater stage, John L. Sullivan made his New York prizefighting debut and there, a year later, became nationally famous by beating Paddy Ryan. Next door was Tony Pastor's theater and club. On its stage Nellie Leonard, the "English ballad singer" from Clinton, Iowa, made her reputation under the name Lillian Russell, a name as redolent of the 1890s as Diamond Jim. For two decades her hourglass figure and regular features established her as the most pictured woman in America. The Bartholdi Hotel, on Madison Square, was another lively sporting and theatrical rendezvous. The prizefighters Bob Fitzsimmons and Kid McCoy were among its star boarders; its bar ran day and night, as did an up-stairs poker game—three tables, no limit. The Hoffman House was a lounging place for sportsmen and stockbrokers, among them James R. Keene and Phil Dwyer. Rector's Restaurant, all red plush and overstuffed patrons, was the favored place for men about town to dine.

Play. Entertainment. Rich visitors descended on New York City to be amused—"copper kings from Butte, silver barons from Denver, cattle princes from Oklahoma, railroad lords from the Northwest, lumber emirs from Michigan, oil rajahs from Texas, pork caliphs from Chicago—bringing their check books with them." They went to the race tracks. They went to the private clubs and casinos run by Richard Canfield and Joe Hall. There were two- and three-day poker parties in John W. "Bet-a-Million" Gates's suite at the Waldorf and dice games in brokers' offices in Wall Street.[5]

That was where Diamond Jim came in. He sensed that business was increasingly connected with entertainment, and he knew that you had to spend money to make it. He was born above a saloon in an Irish neighborhood in Manhattan in 1846, and his father died when he was young. He fled the saloon world (in later life he did not drink), worked as a baggage handler for a railroad, became a salesman and traveled around the country selling railroad supplies at a time of fantastic rail expansion. In the tradition of the "drummer" of Tod Sloan's youth, Jim's life had been on the road. But now, in the 1890s, it was centered in New York City. Customers came to him to conduct business and to be amused, or the other way round.

"If you're going to make money—you've got to look like money" was one of Jim's axioms. In this too he understood his time. Appearances had always mattered, but now photography made one's appearance a democratic possession, and pictures of Jim and Lillian were often in the papers. Everything had a measurable value, and it was agreed that Jim's nickname was the most valuable in the country. To hang back was to get lost. Jim and Lil often went to the Gravesend track, where it became a tradition that Lil posed in the paddock with the winner of the Brooklyn Handicap. In that competition, as was often noted, the horse always took second place. The culture was gross as well as flash. Jim ate immense meals (fourteen courses were not unusual). His gluttony was almost as celebrated as his jewels. Overdressing was another art Jim mastered, outdoing his now-forgotten rivals Evander Berry Wall and Bob Hilliard. In the 1880s Barry Hill's outlandish dress had made him King of the Dudes, a term of wide application; the dude was a favorite low comedy character on the American stage.

Having eaten and drunk, and having been to the theaters and race tracks, the big spenders looked for women. The women were there, "swarms of pretty women" who knew their way about the clubs and theaters and were typically found in the lobbies of the big hotels. Large and lavish hotels were part of this entertainment culture—the Imperial Hotel in 1890, the Holland House in 1891, the Savoy in 1892, the New Netherland Hotel in 1894 (with telephones, a startling luxury). The Old Plaza Hotel was grandly rebuilt, and William Waldorf Astor's Waldorf-Astoria in 1896 became a synonym for the sumptuous. "How those women did dress!" a visitor noted. "And what an eye-

Diamond Jim Brady at the track in the company of
Jesse Lewisohn, at right. Keeneland-Cook.

ful the girls made." He added, "If a fellow could get away from
his wife for an evening and knew somebody who was 'onto the
ropes,' that somebody could produce a bunch of beauts, and,
gosh! They weren't shy at all."[6]

That was also where Diamond Jim came in. He, if anyone,
was onto the ropes, and he supplied women as part of the entertainment. For his more hardboiled clients there was Corey's, on
Sixth Avenue, where the fun was "loud and lusty" and the women
"blonde and beefy." For others he arranged parties in respectable
but broadminded hotels, like the Imperial or Gilsey House.
Sometimes he had as many as five parties going at the same time.
Chorus girls for supper parties? "Easiest thing in the world," Jim
would say. "I'll call up Flo Ziegfeld and he'll have half a dozen
snappy numbers down here for us right after the show." Brady
would meet the women in the lobby of the hotel where the party
was to be, hand each of them a hundred dollar bill, and give instructions. "Sometimes it might be 'kid 'em along and hold their

hand once in a while,' though more often it was 'go as far as you like, girls—and you won't make *me* mad!' "[7]

Some men preferred the company of athletes. Jim could arrange that as well. He paid John L. Sullivan a hundred dollars a night to attend his parties. As soon as Tod Sloan had made a name for himself, "the dandy little jockey hobnobbed with glittering personalities," a turf writer noted. Tod himself later wrote proudly: "I came next to many celebrities in my own land." Tod copied their clothes, learned their manners and style. "He was as much a prima donna as any of the greater figures of the theater with whom he loved to associate," but no one had to pay him anything. Tod became famous for picking up tabs. The (little) Big Spender from the West, the "idol of a city's throngs," became a transatlantic figure, moving easily among the great, and many a wax-mustached New York man about town told stories about him: "We were having a *soupcon* at Rector's when, my word! A little fellow smoking a fat perfecto and wearing the loudest waistcoat swung through the doors and called, 'Drinks for the house!' Tod Sloan. He came straight to me—his head barely topped the bar—and he remarked that the Prince of Wales . . ."[8] It was intoxicating to have so many friends. But friendship, as Tod would find out, could prove dangerous.

The owners of the New York race tracks, famous Wall Street gamblers, were also part of flash culture, their names constantly in the newspapers. Tod Sloan rode for most of them, stayed at their hotels, felt at ease in their presence at the track, though he didn't move in their company socially.

There were two groups. The best known were those plutocrats who emulated the British racing aristocracy. Such was August Belmont I (1816–90), whose unbounded arrogance gained him widespread deference and typified the group members' consciousness of their power to command. Of Belmont it was said that "if he cannot have a thing his own way, he won't touch it at all." William C. Whitney (1841–1904) was unusual because of his involvement in formal national politics as secretary of the Navy in the first Grover Cleveland administration. He didn't become serious about racing until the mid-1890s, after he had left politics; but once he began racing he did so in a dominating manner. When Whitney approached the trainer Samuel Hildreth one afternoon in 1898 to ask him to train at his stable, Hildreth inquired how soon Whitney wanted an answer. The reply was "now." The Lorillard brothers, Pierre (1833–1901) and George (1843–86), who inherited a tobacco fortune from their father, were also yachtsmen, trap shooters, and sulky drivers. Pierre was an internationalist in his racing enterprise, "cutting a wide swath on both sides of the Atlantic." George, less flamboyant, was a more interesting man, a qualified physician, a graduate of Yale Scientific School, genial and well liked, unusual qualities in this group.[9]

Those in the other group could be called the buccaneers. Social outsiders, they didn't disguise their lowly origins. Of these men, James R. Keene (1838–1913) had the longest and most important career in American racing between the Civil War and World War I. A lean, intense man, he was born in London and came to the United States as a boy with his parents, who settled in California; there he worked at a variety of jobs, editing a newspaper and even teaching school, until he made millions in mines in Nevada in the 1870s. He moved to New York, stormed Wall Street with mixed results, began racing, setting himself up as the antagonist first of George Lorillard and then of William Whitney. Keene too was an important transatlantic figure. The career of Marcus Daly (1841–1900) paralleled Keene's. A native of Ireland who emigrated to America as a boy, he worked as a pick-and-shovel miner at fifteen, made his fortune in the Anaconda copper mine in Butte, Montana, then added holdings in railroads, timber, and banks. When he got into New York racing in the 1890s he spent more than a million dollars buying horses.

The Dwyer brothers, Michael (1856–1906) and Philip (1844–1917), were urban buccaneers, born not only on the wrong side of the tracks but on the wrong side of the river, in Brooklyn. They took over and expanded their father's butcher shop and made a great success of the wholesale meat business. Since 1875 they had owned a stable that they operated on the "try before you buy" principle, buying only horses that had been running for someone else. Jesse Lewisohn (1872–1918) moved in and out of Wall Street, theatrical, and racing circles. A member of a wealthy family with interests in banking and copper, he had a stable of horses for a number of years and was a familiar figure at race tracks in the United States and Europe. He could be seen chatting with Tod Sloan and other jockeys, and with trainers and owners of all kinds. He was also a prominent first-nighter at theaters in New York, London, and Paris. He was the constant companion of Lillian Russell for a decade and was an intimate friend of Diamond Jim, an intimacy that eventually caused difficulties. Lewisohn fell in love with Edna McCauley, a New York showgirl who was Brady's mistress at the time. He abandoned Lillian, took Edna away from Jim, and married her and lived in Europe for a number of years.[10]

Different as they were in many ways, the plutocrats and the buccaneers shared a passion for gambling. Keene believed that "any man who bets consistently is a sucker," but he was the "high priest of the ticker," the "greatest stock gambler of his day." Wall Street habitués considered that he didn't do it primarily for the money but rather as a "sportsman, who found in manipulating stocks and bonds the same excitement other sportsmen might get from [horse racing]."[11] Michael Dwyer's betting was so unrestrained that it was rumored that the brothers opened Gravesend track as a way to control his gambling mania. He bet huge amounts on favorites, whatever the odds. Competition, on the Street or at the track, was in the gamblers' blood. They had few scruples about means; whatever led to success justified itself. No one was compelled to take part in racing or on Wall Street; when one did, player or buyer beware.

However, as horse racing became big business, a familiar

paradox arose. Successful play required the opposite of playfulness; it required order and regulation. Racing's nabobs slowly discerned that they had to regulate racing to protect their investments. But they had a morbid dislike of authority other than their own, were congenitally unable to cooperate on equal terms with anyone. Nevertheless, something had to be done, as the example of Chicago made clear. There, the mixture of unregulated competition and political corruption had produced mayhem. There was too much racing. Ed Corrigan, who played an important role in California racing and owned Hawthorne race track on Chicago's outskirts, persuaded the mayor of Chicago to crack down on Garfield track, which was within the city limits. Several hundred police raided Garfield, arresting customers and officials. "Jockeys were loaded into patrol wagons while still wearing their racing silks." A former Texas sheriff who was present refused to accept arrest, and in the gunfight that ensued he killed two policemen before being gunned down himself.[12] Chicago was an extreme example, of course, but everywhere reputable race tracks refused to cooperate with one another. There were no uniform standards or rules. Jockeys and trainers disciplined at one track were often welcome at others. Horses were raced too often. Doping and race-fixing were common.

In 1890, Pierre Lorillard organized a meeting to do something about all this. The result was the establishment of a Board of Control comprising representatives of four New York tracks—Sheepshead Bay, Gravesend, Monmouth Park, and Morris Park—along with three stable owners; the board would regulate racing at those tracks. However, there were various deficiencies in this scheme. Trainers, jockeys, and bookmakers were not represented, and there were serious differences of self-interest between the stable owners and the race track representatives. When they disagreed, the independent stable owners were outvoted. So James R. Keene tried his hand, inviting important owners in the East and Midwest to attend a dinner at the Hoffman House in order to organize a jockey club similar to the one in England. It would be composed primarily of owners "interested in the general welfare of racing rather than the success of particular tracks." This jockey club would allot racing dates, revise rules, appoint officials, license jockeys and trainers, and be a court of appeal on disciplinary matters. The New York Jockey Club came into being in 1893 with seven stewards running it, among them August Belmont and James Keene.[13]

Many people doubted that horsemen could reform themselves, especially when they were businessmen who generally hated reform. Anyway, the debate over horse racing was a small affair compared to the growing clamor that business itself needed reforming. It is a nice coincidence that Lorillard's first effort coincided with a much greater one, the passage of the Sherman Anti-Trust Act of 1890, ineffectual at first but an instrument for later use. Tod Sloan worked in an environment not conducive to moral uplift, but his career would in fact be profoundly affected by the contradictory currents of laissez-faire and reform.

# EIGHT

# MASTERY

Sloan's success in California had meant little to skeptical eastern racing men. New York journalists didn't identify Sloan's forward seat as something radically different but as an exaggerated version of what was already familiar. If anything, it was identified as western or Wild Western, "the reckless cowboy style, admired by spectators and greatly dreaded by other jockeys." It was disconcerting to many. One perturbed racing writer contrasted it with that of the established jockeys of the day, Sims and Griffin, Doggett and Taral, "who ride the same evenly balanced races as of old." The payoff was not in style, however, but in success at the finishing post. In that respect Sloan's performance in the spring and summer of 1896 was modest but noteworthy. His was an unfamiliar name, still often spelled Sloane, and he didn't have a large number of mounts with which to reduce the unfamiliarity, though this may to some extent have been his choice. He did have one advantage—the introduction of a new kind of starting machine, "the latest addition to the collection of starting novelties," introduced at Sheepshead Bay. This one, from California, had wheels and so could be moved easily from pole to pole. There remained much opposition to its introduction, and one writer noted mordantly that "a machine to curb bad acting and non-trying jockeys would certainly prove popular."[1]

Whether from a starting machine or not, Sloan was beginning to get a reputation for fast starts, for getting a jump on his rivals, for stealing races from superior horses. But it wasn't only fast starts. At the same time he was identified with blazing finishes. He won on Haphazard when, after a forty-five minute wait at the starting post (without the machine), "at the end [he] began really riding and made up half a dozen lengths and won by a neck"; or there was his "bringing Oracle up with a rush for a dead heat." Most impressive and important of all, he began to reveal that he had a remarkable sense of pace and of the overall shape of the race, a shrewd ability to estimate his competitors accurately and guess what they would do. On Belmar he rode with "admirable judgment, winning at the post with a well timed drive." He rode a "nice waiting race on Salvado. He sat perfectly still until well within the last sixteenth. Then he [passed the leader], beating him handily by half a length." And there was his victory with Casette, "who ran about the best race she has ever shown, thanks to the fact that she had Sloane in the saddle."[2]

He also began to win races in clusters, the invariable mark of a strong jockey: two winners in one day in May, then doubles again in late June and in July, and then, on July 24, at Brighton Beach, three winners. A further tribute; other jockeys were beginning to imitate the forward seat. Even the racing writer for the *New York Times,* generally dismissive of the work of most jockeys, ended the season with a positive evaluation: "Young Sloane, by the way, has developed wonderfully, and is now one of the very best of the light-weight jockeys."[3]

In 1897, Tod Sloan established himself as a dominant

jockey at any weight, and he became a public favorite. Previous was one of three winners he rode on June 12 at Gravesend, and "when he trotted Previous back to the stand there was no doubt that the victory was popular." Bettors paid him their greatest compliment—backing horses because he was riding. "Sloan won on Domitor and the crowd, believing it was in for a 'Sloan day,' backed everything he rode." When, on July 24, he rode three winners, there was exceptionally vigorous betting on all of them, "on the assumption that the other jockeys would be out-generalled by Sloan at the post and during the race." He won by a nose with Howard Mann, "too close a call for the crowd which had bet heavily on him."[4]

For ordinary racing fans the forward seat was important because it obviously worked and because it was a very visible symbol of Sloan's riding hard to win. It gave a vivid impression of dynamic aggressiveness. "Sloan was punching and riding for dear life at the end to win by half a length." Salazar ran for him "like a seared god." Or: "Sloan rallied the favorite with a final burst." No wonder spectators cheered him. Careful observers noted his growing subtlety, the way he was learning to vary his tactics. In one race he led all the way with Clifford; when another horse passed him all seemed lost. But "Sloan was playing possum [and] . . . called on Clifford who bounded to the front." Even when he didn't win he seemed to be in it. "He hustled Dacian along so strongly that he almost won." In his "imaginative" way, the "wily Sloan," the "wizard," found ways to win. "Previous, like many other horses, ran best for Tod Sloan."[5]

But it wasn't all roses and plaudits. Despite the faith the general bettors had in him, his riding was erratic. There was a puzzling contradiction between the impression he gave of furi-ous activity and of nonchalant carelessness or indifference. At times, "Sloan appeared to regard going to the post as a mere for-mality." "Belleport, the favorite, and ridden by Sloan, was dis-gracefully beaten." "Lady Mitchell should have won easily, but Sloan only woke up at the head of the stretch." "Petrel was

Tod Sloan seemed to make horses win despite
themselves. National Museum of Racing,
Saratoga Springs, New York.

winning but Sloan became overconfident and threw the race
away."[6]

How much of all this was due to Tod Sloan? How much
was the result of the inevitable ambiguity of betting and odds-
making? The Sloan craze was contagious and raised expectations
unreasonably, adding to the general betting frenzy as both cause
and effect. We have a description of a day at Morris Park when
the total bet went over a million dollars, "enough almost to in-
sure the freedom of Cuba, or to bail a king." People in the betting enclosures "surged and jostled upon each other in their ea-
gerness to get their money down." The scene was a "vast financial
whirlpool," much like the stock exchange on a busy day. Tod

should win even with losers and never lose with anything else—
the bettor's fantasy formula. In fact, he still did lose, and, even
with his phenomenal success, he lost more often than he won.
"One of the surest things" at a particular meeting was a horse
with Sloan up, surest only because Sloan was up. They finished
third. Sometimes the Sloan frenzy produced absurd results.
"Sloan was in great demand in the Boulevard Handicap, where
he piloted the bettors' first choice, Voter." But this colt, "strange
as it appeared to his supporters, could not outrun a Tammany
man in a reform district, for he finished absolutely last in a six
horse field." Losing didn't seem to break the Sloan spell. The ir-
rationality of bettors wasn't the jockey's responsibility.

But winning didn't resolve the doubts of those skeptical
about him and his style of riding. Hamburg was Marcus Daly's
horse, perhaps the greatest mount of the first half of the decade,
remarkable for Herculean weight-carrying feats—127, 129, 135
pounds, conceding 25 to 40 pounds to his opponents. Hamburg
was a glutton for work and was so powerful that some horsemen
believed that Sloan wasn't strong enough "to hold such a great
heavy-headed colt." But when Tod rode Hamburg, he won. This
only provoked disdain from the traditionally riding jockey Fred
Taral about Sloan, the forward seat, and Sloan's general success.
"I think anybody could have ridden Hamburg today [and won].
I don't mean any jockey, but any man who knows how to sit on
a horse."[7]

Taral's disparagement is fitting, for the contrast between
him and Sloan not only has to do with traditional versus new
ways of riding, but also with respected and successful jockey versus one who has gone beyond jockeyship to public notoriety.
Taral, the "demon Dutchman," was a workhorse. He accepted
five thousand mounts in his career and won more than one thousand races. He was always "straight as a string," and his "honest
blue eyes mirrored the integrity of his character." Contrast this
with the brilliant, whimsical, and erratic Sloan, cocky and strut-
ting in a way the stolid Taral never would. These two were not,

however, entirely different. Taral was a demon gambler. He and his friend of John L. Sullivan were known as Big and Little Casino.

Sloan's rise to celebrity involved more than his riding. His manner and behavior, off the track as well as on it, both appealed to and annoyed people. He received a phenomenal amount of publicity for a jockey, a little man, a nobody. When he was ill and missed a day's riding, newspapers reported it. When he was involved in a disciplinary action, however routine, there was comment. As a young man, as we've seen, Tod had been briefly attracted to the idea of a career on the stage, in vaudeville—after all, size didn't matter much for dancers and singers—and he now avidly took to theatrical culture and gave full expression to the histrionic aspect of his work: the jockey as performer. Now he was somebody, and he called attention to himself. He bought a boat and took friends out on well-publicized sailing expeditions, "dodging rocks, mud banks, and reckless craft in a manner so seaman-like that his party promptly voted him a commodore." The patronizing tone makes clear that readers were expected to find all this absurdly comic. Yet what better claim did Cornelius Vanderbilt have to be called "commodore"?[8] Did people laugh at *him?*

Tod's clothes were a source of much comment. His "yachting phase" carried over to the race track, where "out before the grand stand, you might have seen yesterday a little chap in duck trousers and coat of blue. His shoes were white, his hat was bound by ribbons of white and palest blue. He was Tod Sloan, jockey and patron of the sea." The number of trunks of clothes that accompanied him on his travels were the cause of much what—merriment? respect? certainly interest. What was perhaps an affectation in others was in him "grandiose behavior." A jockey colleague insisted that Tod changed his clothes between every race.

A number of things that annoyed some people about Tod—his appeal for women, his dandyish dress, the forward seat—are interestingly combined in an otherwise ordinary newspaper story about one day's racing. They form a caustic portrait of the "comic-opera jockey" riding George Keene, a horse that was second favorite "for no reason on earth that was apparent, unless it was that Sloan was in the saddle." In this account Tod "climbed up on the horse's neck regardless of the creases in his satin riding breeches and made a sharp bid for the applause of the gallery and the host of soubrettes who were there to see 'Our Tod' win. 'Toddy' did his best. . . . There were cheers and cries of encouragement for Sloan, in which every chorus girl that could get to the track joined in her shrillest notes. The pride of the San Francisco Tenderloin district responded his prettiest, and worked like a Trojan, for he knew that every 'soubrette' had her week's salary bet on his mount, at 12 to 1." He finished second. After all, then, were they so foolish to bet on him?[9]

There were more serious concerns about Sloan's riding and behavior. He was involved in a number of questionable races. In 1896 he rode Paladin in a race in which a "fortune" was won. Pittsburgh Phil Smith, the well known gambler, was reputed to have taken $50,000 out of the enclosure about him." "The race looked so unreal from a form standpoint that the stewards immediately began an investigation." It was decided that no further entries from that owner would be accepted, but no blame was attached to the jockey, who, after all, won the race. (The decision was greeted with hoots of mockery by writers: "This cannot fail of producing a reformation that will last the week out.") In another race that year, his horse was left at the post, "and Sloane was called up to tell the stewards how it happened." But this sort of thing happened with many jockeys. There were, however, a handful of jockeys who were universally considered straight shooters and were never tainted by suspicion. Tod Sloan was certainly not one of them.[10]

What was not known by the general public was that Sloan had a very special relationship with the most successful of the big-time gamblers of the day, George "Pittsburgh Phil" Smith (1862–1905). There was no doubting Smith's success; at his death he left a fortune estimated at $1 million, thus contravening the most famous of all racing adages by E. Phocian Howard: "All horseplayers die broke." (Strictly speaking, that didn't apply to Howard either, who, when he died, had $2.37 in his pockets, enough for a two-buck bet.) Smith began his working life as a cork cutter in Pittsburgh. He escaped the tedium of factory work by betting on baseball games and then horse races in Chicago pool halls, gathered together some ready cash and went East to study racing. Smith wanted to develop an impersonal, scientific system of betting. Study was the operative word. He was contemptuous of the way most people, including the best-known plungers—Lucky Baldwin, Mike Dwyer, Bet-a-Million Gates—bet their money. "Playing the races appears to be the one business in which men believe they can succeed without special study, special talent, or special exertion." Smith explained his ideas to Edward W. Cole, racing writer for the *New York Evening Telegram,* in what apparently was the only interview he ever gave. (He would "fairly run at the sight of a reporter.") The interview was published in 1908, after Smith's death, as a small booklet titled *Racing Maxims and Methods of "Pittsburgh Phil,"* the "condensed wisdom" of twenty years' experience.[11]

Smith studied horses carefully, especially after a race, to prepare for the horse's next appearance. He also paid attention to the habits and behavior of bookmakers, primarily to keep them in the dark about his own betting; to do this he used an elaborate system of agents, each operating independently of the others, to place his bets. Above all he concentrated on the methods of those who were engaged in the direct control of the horses—the trainers and jockeys. To do this objectively, he kept his distance from owners, trainers, and jockeys (except one), and was patient in analyzing the strengths, limitations, and temperaments of each. "Even that is not good enough. You must know what [the trainer's] methods are with reference to jockeys."

Smith understood that betting on horses was more complex than simply finding out who was honest and who was not, important as that was. He believed that able and honest trainers often unintentionally handicapped their horses by giving jockeys too complicated instructions. "Honest horses ridden by honest boys are oftentimes beaten by honest trainers."[12]

In Pittsburgh Phil's *Maxims* there is a chapter about his special relationship with Tod Sloan. This material was not provided by Smith but was written by Cole after Smith's death. What it recounts may have come directly from Smith; Cole insisted that it did, but we can't be sure. Whatever its source, it contains an extraordinary revelation about the jockey and the plunger. According to Cole's account, Smith and Sloan met at the Bay District track at the beginning of Tod's riding career. The racing there, in Pittsburgh Phil's opinion, was so crooked that a "cold deliberating handicapper, who depended upon form for his deductions, was a victim at almost every turn." Smith was so disgusted by this situation that he had made up his mind to leave California. "Three and four horses in a race were being taken care of by their riders in the interests of their employers." Cole's account doesn't go into detail about the extent of Sloan's involvement in this, but it suggests a good deal. "In those days Sloan was hustling his way through the world as best he could, putting a bet down for himself when he had the money, and when he was without, doing his best to get someone to make a wager for him."[13]

As a result of their meeting, Smith proposed to Sloan that he reform the erratic way he had been riding, become thorough in his work, and ride to win from the drop of the starter's flag. In return, Smith promised to pay Sloan $400 every time he rode a winner, whether or not Smith bet on Sloan's horse. Smith was insistent on being clear about this; he was not committing himself to bet on Sloan's mounts unless his calculations showed him they were superior. The only condition to the agreement was that there be absolute secrecy about it. "The only two things that you have to think about," Cole reported Smith as saying, "are winning a race and collecting $400 for so doing." And he added, "That is more money than you can make mixing up with 'sharps' and you will get your money." The benefits for Sloan were obvious. What was in it for Smith? Given the prevailing dishonesty, it was crucial for him to know that there was one jockey "trying to win every race against half a dozen who were manipulating horses at the dictation of unscrupulous owners and trainers."[14]

This account is supplemented by a series of three articles dictated to the racing writer and broadcaster Clem McCarthy by Pittsburgh Phil's nephew three decades after Smith's death. The nephew, James C. McGill, said that he was at his uncle's side morning and night the last ten years of his life, and his articles are filled with lively and persuasive detail, especially about the Tod Sloan connection and arrangement. His account substanti-

The cool and calculating George "Pittsburgh Phil" Smith studied horses and riders carefully and had a special relationship with Tod Sloan.

ates the original chapter in *Maxims.* What Pittsburgh Phil saw of Tod Sloan's riding in San Francisco impressed him; he liked Sloan's forward crouch, his knack of keeping a mount out of trouble, the timing of his final move. Sloan was remarkable at making sulky horses run well, and he often won very close finishes. In those days Sloan had the arms and shoulders of a man thirty pounds heavier than his ninety or so pounds and thus was in as good control of his horses as men heavier than he.[15]

The Sloan-Smith arrangement, McGill wrote, proved a bonanza for both men. Because he could concentrate on his riding and not be tempted by "offers" from others or by proposed hanky-panky, Sloan began to win consistently. "No other jockey, before or since, has been the sensation that Tod was in the ensuing two years." And they were, not coincidentally, the most profitable betting years Pittsburgh Phil ever had. Certainly, the story, in both versions, dovetails with the outline of Sloan's career as we have followed it. Smith was in California in the Sloan years, and it is highly likely that they would have met in some circumstances or other. Smith was perceptive enough to see that Sloan had found a way to win, *if he tried,* that is to say, if his primary interest was in winning.

Many aspects of the Sloan-Smith partnership are puzzling. For instance, it would seem to have made sense for Smith, onto a very good thing, to have urged Tod to go East and make his reputation and their joint fortunes. Perhaps he did so, but Tod's recollection was the reverse of this. "It's a different game there son," Tod later quoted him as saying. "You are known here [in California], and you have confidence in yourself, but you'll find it a cold proposition there." Was this paternal or avuncular anxiety on Smith's part? A sudden loss of confidence, or some other subtle game he was playing? Tod's response, in his memoirs, was crisply confident. "I have made up my mind to go . . . and when the flag falls at Morris Park, you'll find me on deck." But Pittsburgh Phil did more than find him on deck. In the East, Smith and Sloan openly lived together for the next year, a relationship—jockey and professional gambler—that was neither prohibited nor even frowned upon at the time, but which, within a few years, would have resulted in the jockey's banishment from racing.[16]

The arrangement came to an end. Smith became unhappy with Sloan's inability to stand prosperity. Even Sloan's closest friends "couldn't get the little rider to bed early or bring him out to the track for an important trial unless Sloan was in the mood." And there were "leaks" in the arrangement; people imposed on Sloan's "notorious generosity." The greatest effect of this arrangement may have been to confirm Tod's feeling that he could do as he wished without risk.[17]

Pittsburgh Phil's account of his betting career and the nephew's admiring narrative both, unsurprisingly, present us with the classic, imperturbable, poker-faced gambler: "He could watch a nose finish, be standing to win or lose a fortune on it, but never blink an eye, snap his fingers or utter a sound." Here is the scientific odds-maker, untouched by the sordid crookedness that surrounded horse racing. In fact, Smith's career was far from sanitary, and his operations were very much part of the contemporary gambling ethos. In his quest for more information from horsemen he was said to have spent at least $1,000 per day on stable boys, trainers, jockeys, clockers; he distributed "commissions" lavishly in the betting enclosures for whatever purpose suited him. Nor was he impartial. He owned horses that he ran and on which he bet; and, for all anyone knows, bet against. And after all, whatever was included in the Sloan-Smith arrangement beyond what was revealed, like so much of this story, took place in the shadows.

Nor was he an interesting man; his nephew admitted that his uncle thought of little but horses. He never married, never traveled, never indulged himself—except at the end. He died of tuberculosis but left money in his will for the erection, in a Pittsburgh cemetery, of a $30,000 marble monument: a likeness of himself standing above the pediment, in a frock coat, holding a racing program card in his hand. Horse players believed he died of ice water in the veins.

In 1898, Todd Sloan "continued his victorious career." He became familiar with the "mad burst of cheering at the finish line," and he seemed to make horses win despite themselves, "landing a faint-hearted filly in front by a head"; in another, "snatching victory out of defeat in the last stride." The clusters of first-place finishes came thick and fast. On May 12 the headlines blared: SLOAN WON THREE RACES; the next day he won twice and finished second three times, and on the 15th he won twice and had a place and a show. Two firsts on the 17th and two more on the 18th. On May 21 he won the Eclipse Stakes with Geisha and the National Stallion Stakes, for the huge purse of $20,000, with Jean Bereaud. That was an example of superb coolness. After a delay at the post of twenty-six minutes the horses were off; within a few strides Sloan lost a stirrup, but he collected himself and caught the leader, then gave Jean Bereaud a "gentle cut" and his mount "shot away as if [the rest] were standing still." May 28, at Gravesend, was marked by a magnificent FIVE WINNERS in one day. June and July were equally brilliant, with a steady stream of victories dotted with outcroppings of two and three winners in a day. His dominance was remarkable. At the June meeting of the Coney Island Jockey Club eighty races were run. No jockey won more than seven, other than Sloan, who won twenty-six.[18]

An occasional writer tried to restore some balance and managed only to sound churlish: "The fact that Sloan was on Ogden caused the odds against him, 4–1, to be shorter than otherwise, the public at large having apparently made an idol of this jockey, backing his every mount; but while Sloan rode a well-judged race, Ogden's performance was due to his quality, not to his jockey's." The public paid no attention. Sloan felt that 1898 was, in many respects, the apex of his career—up to that point. The forward crouch had swept opposition aside; all the younger jockeys copied it and pushed it further.

All of this, at age twenty-three, no doubt was very satisfying. Yet it seems that Tod dreamed of something else. Perhaps it wasn't something as clear as a dream but was rather vague. Perhaps he strained against his destiny as a man enclosed in a boy's body. "I had got as far as I could get in the way of riding success," he wrote later, looking back at these years, "and I was longing to achieve something in another walk of life."[19] He had had a taste of something else, something new, in the fall of 1897, racing in England.

# NINE

# ENGLAND

In the late summer of 1897, James R. Keene and Tod Sloan had a conversation. Like so many things in Sloan's life, there is uncertainty about what was said; or, rather, there are two distinct versions of it. Each gives a glimpse of one of his many moods and manners. In Sloan's own version Keene had sent for him. "Sloan, I've got a horse, St. Cloud, in the Cesarwitch and the Cambridgeshire. My trainer, Pincus, thinks he has a good chance. I have been thinking over the advantage of getting you to ride him. Would you like to go over to England?" Tod remembered that it didn't take him long to reply: "I certainly would."

The other version is from Foxhall Keene, James Keene's son. "On a day in September, 1897, a person dressed in flaming raimant, with a cigar a foot long between his teeth, strolled nonchalantly past an over-awed secretary, straight into my father's private office." This apparition introduced himself: "I'm Tod

Sloan and I want to ride St. Cloud in the Cesarwitch and Cambridgeshire."

He was the no-nonsense professional weighing a proposal. He was also the bumptious little man of breezy effrontery, coolly dictating terms to a Wall Street titan. (We wish we knew, in version two, what Keene said.) In any event, both Keene and Sloan were gamblers used to taking chances. It didn't take Tod long to get ready to leave on what would turn out to be the first chapter of a great adventure. He sailed on September 29 and in doing so crisscrossed one of the major themes of nineteenth-century American culture, the transatlantic relationship with Britain and Europe.[1]

Transatlantic sports had been a one-way affair: Americans imported British games and sports. Some were accepted unchanged, some adapted to different interests, some eventually rejected. Cricket, for example, was a game with a considerable American following in the 1840s and 1850s, a game preserved as nearly as possible in its original form. However, the Civil War intensified nationalistic feeling. Cricket wasn't Americanized; it was displaced by baseball, which, itself a version of an English import, rounders, was then hailed as the distinctive national game. Rugby and soccer came to the United States in the mid-nineteenth century, primarily to American colleges. There followed a gradual amalgamation of the two, out of which came something distinctive, American football. The importation of English games accelerated in the last third of the century: crew and croquet, tennis and golf, all absorbed in their original form.

In three long-established sports—sailing, prizefighting, and horse racing—the relationship between the two sporting cultures had a different twist. In all three, Americans attempted to maintain British forms and traditions, and in all three they also began to challenge the British in direct competition. In the summer of 1850, John Cox Stevens sailed his yacht, *America,* to the Isle of Wight and defeated the yachtsmen there in surprising fashion. As a trophy of his victory Stevens was presented with an ornately ugly cup, thereafter known as the America's Cup, which subsequently became the object of sporadic but intense competition, remarkable for its sustained tradition of rancor and bad sportsmanship.

Prizefighting, for Americans, was one of the "unexpected blessings of independence." British sailors introduced it to the colonists during the Revolutionary War; it flourished in the same harsh and brutal conditions of lower-class life in America as in Britain. Although it was illegal it spread widely; some of its appeal, no doubt, was due to the fact that it *was* illegal. For many years it was too disreputable to gain much public notice, but for half a century American fighters went to Britain to take on the champions there: Tom Molineaux, an African American, fought Tom Cribb in 1810 with very little notice, while in 1860, John C. Heenan, the Benicia Boy, fought the Englishman Tom Sayers in a much-publicized and long-remembered match.

Thereafter the transatlantic rivalry declined. Prizefighting retained a substantial following in the United States. The career of the last and most famous of the bare-knuckle breed, John L. Sullivan, brings us down to the time of Tod Sloan. By the 1880s it became clear that reform was necessary if prizefighting was to become commercially lucrative. Reform came with one final importation from England, a new set of rules—gloves, a fixed number of rounds, each of a fixed duration—the Marquess of Queensbury's rules of 1882.

Horse racing was the most venerable of the imported British sports. Although few Americans knew much of it by direct experience, it was part of their historical inheritance. As a result, Americans had only vague ideas about it, usually exalted ones. Contrary to prevailing American stereotypes about British order and decorum, British horse racing in that first half of the century had been a disorderly affair. A police inspector of the day described race meetings as "nothing else than carnivals of drunkenness, crime and misery." British racing spectators were sharply divided by class; it was the sport of the aristocracy and of the lower classes. The middle class was not much represented because respectable opinion disapproved of a sport that wickedly appealed only to "the idle rich and the idle poor."

The Derby was the most famous horse race in the world. Derby day, at Epsom, England, was very different from how most Americans imagined it. It had no parallel in horse racing in America—or anywhere else, for that mater. It was a kind of national holiday, festival, and carnival, a long-anticipated day for unbuttoned amusement. Many local workers were guaranteed that day off; behavior not tolerated elsewhere and at other times, was winked at. "Thousands came for the raciness and not for the racing."[2]

In the last half of the nineteenth century the organization of British racing became more businesslike and its atmosphere—excepting the Derby—more restrained. Race courses were enclosed so that spectators had to pay to enter, which reduced the rowdy element. As railroads speeded horses and people to the more prestigious race courses, the smaller, less formal ones declined in importance. Gambling and drinking were more effectively controlled, and more of the respectable middle class felt it now possible to attend meetings.

One aspect of British racing had not changed: the dominance of the aristocracy. For Americans, certainly for Tod Sloan, this was an essential element in its historic appeal, its contemporary glamour. At a distance, and no doubt idealized in conception, the aristocratic patrons of the turf represented the sportsmen who raced for sport and not for money. Of course they "wanted success and they wanted it quickly," but they knew horses, loved horses, bred them, raised them, didn't simply go into the market to buy them. Races, by now venerable with age, especially compared with the rawness of the American scene, bore their family names or the names of their country houses, which, with their sweeping lawns and splendid stables, glittered and gleamed across the Atlantic as a symbol of the old and authentic. And they were rich, rich enough to indulge in splendid patrician gestures. In 1889, for instance, the Duke of Portland won £80,000 (about $500,000) in that year's racing, and gave it all to charity.

Beyond and above the titled families was the monarchy, the personified reality of the "sports of kings." In late Victorian days this meant Edward, Prince of Wales. Queen Victoria took no interest in racing, rather disapproved of it. Through the protracted unfolding (sixty-four years in all) of his mother's rein, Edward waited and waited to inherit the throne. As he waited, he amused himself. He had "vast opportunities for self-indulgence which he rarely failed to take advantage of." Solitude frightened him; he disliked books. Easily bored, given to bursts of anger that quickly gave way to charming amiability and informality, he added showmanship to the stylish luxury he lived in. "His pleasures became fashion and his whims became policies." People copied what he did and wore. Edward did not mind changing his clothes half a dozen times a day; he never traveled with fewer than two valets, and two more were left behind, cleaning and pressing his clothes. He adored the company of pretty women, wished to be surrounded by them, made love to many. All this of course meant that many of his contemporaries regarded him with disdain, as a superficial and self-indulgent love machine. The slender crown prince of mid-century became, in his last decade, in Rudyard Kipling's words, a "corpulent voluptuary."

With the great mass of people, however, Edward enjoyed a rising tide of approval in the mid-nineties. His ease of manner gained him favor; his circle of acquaintance became more democratic—American heiresses (if pretty), opera singers, actresses, Jews, industrialists, professional beauties. Only one group was taboo: writers, poets, anyone "intellectual." Said Lady Warwick, one of his favorites, "We did not like brains." This didn't work to his discredit with the general public. Nor did his sexual affairs. His vices were private but well known. As sometimes happens, his failings added to his popularity. "The King is loved because he has all the faults of which the Englishman is accused."[3]

There was one thing above all that Edward could share with many of his subjects—horse racing. He knew about horses and cared about them. Someone said that the prince paid attention to young and promising politicians in the same way he paid attention to possible Derby winners in his stable. He organized his stables in the 1870s and was serious about how well the horses did; because he was extravagant in so many ways, the money he made from racing was important to him. Between 1887 and 1907 he estimated that he had made £250,000. His colors, purple, scarlet, and gold, were recognized everywhere. He attended race meetings regularly and, just at the time Tod Sloan came to England, had reached a new level of popularity.

Eighteen ninety-six was a great year for Edward. Persimmon won the Derby and the St. Leger and the Jockey Club Stakes for him. The Derby victory gained him £30,000 in prize money and bets. As Edward led Persimmon into the victory circle after the Derby there was an explosion of popular feeling; hats and canes were thrown in the air. The prince went on to further success, winning the Derby again in 1900 with Diamond Jubilee and a third time in 1909, this time as king, with Minoru, occasioning another outburst of popular support. "Good old Teddy" became a darling of the masses. He was, in addition, a good sport, not blaming others when his horses lost, recognizing how much success depended on luck, what he called the "glorious incertitude of the turf."[4]

One final development sets the racing stage for Tod Sloan's appearance on it: the rise to unquestioned dominance of the Jockey Club, founded in about 1750 by a group of racing men in Newmarket. As Newmarket grew in importance in English racing, so did the Jockey Club, as an impartial and knowledgeable group that could settle disputes. In 1791 an incident immensely increased the Jockey Club's prestige. A horse owned by the then Prince of Wales was ridden so erratically that the prince's favored jockey, Sam Chifney, was thought to deserve severe censure. The Jockey Club proceeded with characteristic in-

The Prince of Wales leading his 1896 Derby winner, Persimmon,
into the winner's circle. During this era the royal family's popularity
was at a high point.

direction. It informed the prince that if Chifney ever rode one
of his horses again, "no gentleman would start against him." The
prince was furious; as a sign of his contempt for the Jockey Club
he settled an annuity of 200 guineas on Chifney. Nevertheless,
the Jockey Club had its way; the prince never again raced his
horses at Newmarket.[5]

In the early nineteenth century the Jockey Club published
its own rules of racing and, after 1807, the *Racing Calendar,* its
official journal, in which it explained its decisions in contro-
verted cases. In the decades that followed the Jockey Club extended its influence and power. Jockeys and trainers obtained a
license only by accepting the convention that the Jockey Club
could withdraw it at any time without a reason being given.
Arrangements were made with foreign jockey clubs, which
agreed to abide by its decisions. The rough gambling element
"didn't give a damn about the Jockey Club," but it also had no
influence to oppose it. Nor was it feasible to challenge it in the
courts or in Parliament.

The Jockey Club's power was essentially personal and so-cial, based on the status of its members and on their intricate net-work of close associations with almost everyone who mattered in the racing and public life of the time. By the late nineteenth century it numbered about one hundred members, including nine stewards who determined policy. The Jockey Club resisted outside influence. "Press publicity served only to close Jockey Club ranks and there was a sturdy refusal to even comment on external criticism." Membership was highly prized, difficult to achieve. A wealthy businessman said that "to become a member you have to be a relative of God—and a close one at that." The men who ran the Jockey Club and who governed racing in Britain were used to governing. There was no formal opposition to it, and had there been, it would have made little difference. "The Jockey Club knew it was right."[6]

Such was the British racing situation when American horsemen began their first challenge to the British on their own turf. In 1854, Richard Ten Broeck, a remarkable horseman and entrepreneur with much racing experience in New York and throughout the South, took a stable of American horses to En-gland. The American Invasion, the British called it. Initially, Ten Broeck had a run of bad luck. Two of his horses died, and his American jockeys couldn't adjust to English conditions and courses. Ten Broeck persevered. He won the Cesarwitch at New-market with Prioress in 1857; the Goodwood Stakes with Um-pire in 1859; the Goodwood Cup in 1861 with Starke. And Um-pire ran second in the Derby. Ten Broeck stayed ten years and became popular with the British, an American "typical of the shrewd, dry, humorous American that one reads of in the novels of Mark Twain."[7] By the time he returned to America he had been forgotten—a civil war had intervened, after all—and so had the American Invasion.

Still, a precedent had been set. Milton Sanford took a num-ber of horses to England in the 1870s. In 1878, Pierre Lorillard launched a very successful campaign: Parole won five of eleven starts, among them the Newmarket Handicap, the Great Metropolitan, and the Epsom Gold Cup. In 1881, Lorillard's Iroquois won seven of nine starts, including the St. Leger and, most memorably, the Derby, defeating a field of fifteen. That same year James R. Keene took his three-year-old, Foxhall (named for his son), to France and England. At Newmarket, Foxhall won the Cesarwitch and beat an outstanding field in the Cambridgeshire.

On that visit Richard Ten Broeck served as Keene's adviser. So the line from Ten Broeck to Keene to Sloan was direct. But there were important differences. These American owners were admired for their personal qualities and because they represented a class and type familiar to the British.[8] Tod Sloan represented something else, a kind of American harder to accept, and of a class so lowly as to be out of conventional social consideration. Nevertheless, forty-three years after Ten Broeck's first assault on the British turf, Tod Sloan would soon find himself at the center of a second American Invasion.

# TEN

# MONKEY SEAT

Tod Sloan's first experience of England, however, wasn't the thrill of invasion, it was loneliness. Keene and Ten Broeck and Lorillard were men with social connections. Sloan, though he had brought a companion with him, was, as always, on his own; he knew "absolutely no one and felt as lonely and out of the swim as a fish on land." He consoled himself by taking rooms at the Savoy Hotel—he always traveled first class—but roamed its corridors "so homesick I nearly cried. I found myself looking at steamship time-tables." Then he went to Newmarket and looked up Jake Pincus, Keene's trainer, an American by birth and a former jockey who had trained Lorillard's horses in the 1870s. Pincus had stayed in England and, Tod felt, "by long residence been turned into a regular Britisher." He was distinctly cool to Sloan and believed that his ignorance of English horses and courses would prove a fatal handicap. Nevertheless, Sloan got some mounts in addition to those he would ride for Keene.[1]

In early October 1897 the New York correspondent for the London *Sporting Life* wrote a piece explaining to British readers what might be expected from the American newcomer. The writer immediately got to the main issue: Tod Sloan's style of riding. It was an "exaggeration" of the short stirrup style used by other Americans. "He lies along his horse's neck like nothing so much as one of those monkeys on a pole that children play with."

There it was, Tod Sloan's passport to international notoriety and then fame! The "monkey on a stick," the monkey seat would forever be associated with him. The writer guessed what a commotion would ensue and that it might dwarf Sloan's talents. "You will say at once that no one can ride like that." But James Keene had been right to choose him. "He is a wonderfully successful jockey," America's premier "lightweight." He excelled in "getting away well," sat "very light" on his horse, was "perfectly motionless" once under way. Was he successful because of his style of riding or despite it? Time alone would tell.[2]

Sloan began by working out on Newmarket Heath. An English sporting journalist recalled a scene there. "I saw coming along a horse with a jockey seated—more or less seated—on his withers. The spectacle was remarkable." The journalist later spoke about this to an English jockey who told him the "apparition was an American jockey named Sloan, who had adopted that "extraordinary" seat, "which was of course quite preposterous." The English jockey then gave an imitation of the invader clutching his reins within a few inches of the bit. "But all the same he can ride!" the jockey observed.[3]

Sloan's first race at Newmarket, as a contemporary recalled it later, was on Quibble II, who had run four times without getting in the money and was a "very bad animal." "Sloan, however, jumped off on him, none of the others got near, and he won by half a dozen lengths." Win or no win, the chorus of ridicule was resounding. "His position on a horse is almost indescribable, and

An English caricature of Tod Sloan in the forward seat. "His position
on a horse is almost indescribable, and we never saw anything like it
outside a circus."

we never saw anything like it outside a circus. He appears to be
on the horse's neck, and to be whispering into his left ear." In his
memoirs Tod admitted that it bothered him when a "big laugh
went up." The next day he was up on the "unconsidered" filly
Jiffy II in the Old Nursery Stakes. The odds were 100–8 against
her. "She won comfortably."[4]

Everything didn't go smoothly, however, which was not
surprising; as another American rider said, "It takes a jockey
some time to adapt himself to new courses and conditions." This
proved to be the case in the Cambridgeshire, one of the races
Sloan had been brought over specifically to ride in. On Keene's
St. Cloud II in a hotly contested struggle among four horses,
Sloan seemed to have it won, only to be beaten by a head, by
Comfrey. Some observers thought he misjudged the finish line
and pulled up; others said that, confused by the width of the
Newmarket course, he lost sight of Comfrey, thought he had
won, and didn't drive hard enough. "So close was the finish," *The*

*Times* reported, "that only heads separated the first four." Another writer observed that "Sloan ought to have made assurance doubly sure, but he rode a good race and was not beaten through incapacity. Such mistakes will occur." The *Sporting Life* writer, describing the race as "one of the best handicaps ever put before the public," thought the race had great significance. It was an "exhibition of two very different styles of race-riding," he wrote, pinpointing a serious flaw in the American style. "If the American method may possibly have its advantage in driving runners quickly away from the post," this line of argument went, "very few who saw the last few strides of this finish would declare against the English system of sitting down in the saddle for the final tussle." Not finishing a race in the proper fashion would be a charge tenaciously held against the monkey on a stick, even though it was a winning style. But whether or not he had finished well, the *Sporting Life* critic insisted that "it would be unfair to withhold the credit of handling his mount in masterly style from Tod Sloan."[5]

Two days later, he rode again. Liberal odds were laid against Sloan's mounts. He rode Meta II for Lord William Beresford, one of the leading figures of the contemporary English turf, Sloan's chief English patron in the early days, and a proponent of the American style of riding and racing. (Beresford had another American racing connection; he formed a partnership with Pierre Lorillard and "with Sloan as their jockey, they had a royal time.") "People were inclined to believe that Lord William was making a mistake when he threw in his lot with the Transatlantic style." "It was indeed a bold thing to depart from tradition." This race was the Free Handicap, and Meta II's chief rival was Jeddah, who was to win the Derby in 1898. It was an exciting race, and with a "desperate effort" Sloan and Meta II got the win by a head. "Unfortunately for us," wrote Richard Marsh, Jeddah's trainer, "this was an occasion when Sloan displayed that genius which made him such a marvelous jockey. I do not pretend to know how he did it but somehow he got up to beat us. . . . The way I

A contemporary English painting titled "Tommy and Toddy." Tommy was Tom Loates, "whose style, however elegant, could not survive against the American, however grotesque."

looked at it was that Sloan, rather than his mount, had beaten Jeddah." Meta II never won again. Sloan had a second mount that day, on Sandia in the Old Cambridgeshire, and won once more "in the most workmanlike style imaginable."[6]

On to Lincoln, where he won the Great Tom Stakes on Angelina at 10–1 and the Great Lancashire Handicap on Easter Gift at the same price. The season ended at Manchester, where Sloan won the Rothschild Plate, "the biggest thing I had done in England." On a Saturday, before a huge crowd, he won the Farewell Handicap with Manxman in a crowded field of fourteen. "They gave me a bit of a cheer." He rode in the next race and won, then won again, and as he passed the finish line the third time, the crowd sent up a roar. He next finished second and then won again. Four wins and a second place!

He changed his clothes and went out to find a carriage. He was astonished to find thousands of people waiting for him, "either to shake my hand or pat me on the back or to grab a souvenir." For a moment, as the crowd closed in on him, he thought that he would be trampled. "I was such a little fellow that I might have been dead while they were looking for me on the ground."

A dozen policemen formed a square around him. All the way back to London he heard the crowd calling his names—"Tod," "Toddie," "Sloan," "Sloanie," and "everything they could twist my name into." He found admiration for his skill: "as warm, hearty, disinterested applause as ever greeted a popular, home-bred idol"; and affection for his person: "The little man came here, was seen and conquered us." His campaign the first year was an abbreviated one; he left England in November to go to California for the winter racing, but he promised to return. All told he rode in fifty-three races and won twenty. His winning percentage was a startling 37 percent. (Good jockeys did well to win 20 percent of the time.) The estimate of *The Times* was judicious but firm: "He has done wonders during the short time he has been riding, and brought the season to what must be regarded as a triumphant close."[7]

In 1898 commitments in California and the East kept Sloan in the United States until September, when he went to Newmarket for the series of three weekly meetings. His success the previous year hadn't convinced the bookmakers, who laid odds of 100–12 against him in his first race. He beat a dozen competitors with Buckbread, then won the other race in which he had a mount. The next day he won twice out of three times, and the day after that three of four. The fifth day was unforgettable. Second by a head in the first race, Tod won four straight races and concluded what he called a "pretty good day's work" by winning the Newcastle St. Leger, his fifth consecutive victory. That day was "absolutely a Sloan one, if one may use the expression for the famous American jockey." Sixteen races, a dozen wins. "No such performance had ever previously been achieved."[8]

In a remarkably short time he had become established. "He seems to stride through form and fashion and put [the odds] at defiance." And he was well liked: "a very popular reception." Even a century later the statistics jump out. At the second Newmarket meeting he won eight races of sixteen, "in nearly every case it is to be noticed by substantial margins." At the third meeting he added seven victories. His Newmarket totals: sixty-three mounts, twenty-seven winners.[9]

Then on to Liverpool and Manchester and more triumphs. Nothing fazed Sloan, who felt confident enough on foreign courses "to remove his field of operations to the Parisian race course at Longchamps," finishing third in the race for the Municipal Prize. Included among his victories was an especially satisfying one when, "as usual, he made the best of his opportunities" and won the Middle Park Plate on Caimon, defeating Flying Fox, one of the outstanding horses of the decade. Tod didn't win the race, he stole it. "Sloan's sharpness and skill were asserted in a fashion that can only be described as astonishing to onlookers and confounding to his rivals."[10] In this second season he registered forty-three victories out of ninety-eight attempts, his winning percentage an astounding 44 percent.

And it was this second season that marked the victory of the monkey seat. The tide had turned. "Whereas hitherto the monkey-like style had been looked upon with ridicule amongst owners and trainers, they are at last compelled to recognize that there is something in it." That recognition was still grudging; the American style would remain a "bone of contention amongst sticklers for the old customs." But the proof was in the winning. "It is useless to deride the style and methods of a jockey who keeps winning." There was no point in picking out bits and pieces of the Sloan style: "If we are to adopt the American plan, we shall have to do so in every detail." And already British jockeys *were* adopting it. "I have seen several little lads riding in Sloan's style, and they seem to get on wonderfully well."[11]

And so, in the fall of 1898, there unfolded the climax of the second, the English, chapter of the story of the forward seat. Two hundred years of English riding were overturned in what seemed no time at all. Diehards continued to insist for years that a "system which had stood the test of many generations may safely be relied upon to come into its own again, when the craze

Tod Sloan, ready for work. An English observer
said of him: "Yes, that there Sloan is mustard.
What he don't know isn't worth picking up, but he
can ride." Keeneland Library.

for a new fashion has worn itself out." But the great and increasing majority of horsemen and writers understood that a
new era had begun. They didn't argue that Tod Sloan had invented this American sport. Some remembered Willie Simms,
who in April 1895 won a race on Eau Gallie, riding in a way that
"vastly amused" observers. "We may as well have this right," a
writer insisted some years later. "Sloan popularized the seat [but]
it was introduced by Simms." And who was to say, or who to care,

where Simms had got it? In any event, Simms won four of nineteen races in England before returning to the United States, and "he never came back."

Now Tod Sloan was vividly present and winning and winning and winning again. Winning was everything, as it always is. Winning was what transformed the new style from a source of derision into an admirable and much-copied innovation. Sloan's triumphs obliterated curiosity about the more distant origin of things. When one English writer ventured the notion that some English riders had actually ridden in a similar fashion, "though not in such a huddled manner," that idea interested no one. "Be that as it may, it was due more to Sloan . . . that this seat came into general use." Anyway, Tod Sloan's success was due to much more than a style of riding. "Sloan measures his winning post with an accuracy which skill and knowledge of pace alone can give," wrote one reporter. And another: "All unprejudiced observers must allow that Sloan is an artist in his own line." There would come a time when Sloan's achievements would be seen as "the most important step in the improvement of the art of race-riding."[12]

So attractive were his prospects and so rewarding his successes in England that Sloan spent the entire 1899 season there. Once again he was triumphant at Newmarket, winning eight of the thirteen races he took part in; on the last day he was up four times without a loss. He won the Thousand Guineas with Lord William Beresford's Sibola but he also lost the Oaks, one of the classic English races, on the same horse, by a nose, in a race that was one of the few genuinely bad examples of riding by him. ("It was the worst race I ever rode in my life.") He lost the Lincoln Handicap as well, another race he was expected to win.[13]

Undoubtedly his greatest disappointment was in a race he was not expected to win but which he was confident he could win—the Derby. Flying Fox was the overwhelming favorite and acknowledged to be the superior entrant. Tod had his heart set

on winning a Derby, the "greatest race in the world." Years later
he reflected on the matter. "In America, even those who do not
follow English racing results will always read anything about the
Derby. I know that *I* did and I often found others doing so." His
horse was Holocaust, a French horse that he had never ridden or
even seen. Could Holocaust win? Only if bad luck came Flying
Fox's way. And that is just what happened. Holocaust stood "as
quiet as a sheep" at the post while six consecutive false starts took
place, with Flying Fox running hard after each one. Sloan calcu-
lated that he ran a mile and a quarter before the race even started.
Then they were off, and sure enough Sloan saw Flying Fox's
jockey go to his whip immediately, for the splendid animal had
been badly tired by the extra running. Here was a race—*the*
race—that Tod could steal. With a furlong and a half to go,
Holocaust pushed his nose in front, and Tod was then, and forever after, convinced that he had Flying Fox beaten. Suddenly
there was a terrible shock, and Holocaust rolled from side to side
and then fell. He had broken his leg. The field thundered by, and
with it Sloan's only real chance to win the Derby. (The next year
he finished third with Disguise II.) There was great controversy
as to which horse would have won had there been no accident.
Inevitably, some observers argued that the monkey seat was the
cause of Holocaust's breakdown. Then and later, the prevailing
opinion was that the magnificent Flying Fox would surely have
come back to win over the "coarse and common" Holocaust; and
that Sloan's insistence that "he had got Flying Fox beaten" was
only another instance of Yankee boasting. Yet there was reputable English support for Sloan's view. George Lambton, a
knowledgeable English trainer who had money bet on Flying
Fox, agreed with Sloan and had "so often heard it said by jockeys" that he didn't think it a questionable view. And Arthur
Coventry, the Jockey Club starter, who was "not too partial to
Sloan, or to the new style of riding which he had introduced,"
when told Sloan's opinion said: "By God, it's true." After the
start, which he had supervised from horseback, Coventry gal-

loped to a place on the rail just a few yards from the spot where Holocaust fell, "and in his opinion Sloan had won the race." But what might have been only added to Tod's anguish. "It is the ambition of every jockey to win a Derby, and that I had the chance of doing so at the first attempt is almost too much to chew over."[14]

Despite such disappointments, 1899 was a banner year. Those who had believed that Sloan's two short previous campaigns in England had reached a rate of success that could not be sustained for a full year's racing—"that he will maintain his average during the coming season seems in the highest degree improbable"—had to reckon with the following end-of-the-year totals: 108 winners out of 345 races, a winning percentage of 31 percent.[15]

Nothing spoiled Sloan's most magical moment of all, "the greatest surprise of my life." He was introduced to Edward, Prince of Wales. One day in 1898 at Newmarket word came that the prince wished to see Tod, who hurriedly put a coat over his riding clothes and was ushered into the royal presence. "He smiled as I came towards him and shook my hand very warmly. Never in my life have I been put so much at my ease nor treated so splendidly. After all, I was only a visiting American, and only a jockey at that." The prince asked him questions. Was he happy? Did he like riding on grass courses? "I felt as if I'd like to talk to him the entire afternoon." And just before the prince left he said that "I should ride for him some time or other, and he gave me time to answer: 'It would be a pride and honour to do so.' "[16]

This led to a mount on the prince's Nunsuch. Tod bungled it. He and four other jockeys were still walking their horses toward the starting line when the starter dropped his flag. Nunsuch never had a chance. When Tod was brought to the prince after the race, Edward was smiling. "Well, such things do happen and it cannot be helped; I will start Nunsuch in the Old Cambridgeshire the day after tomorrow and you shall ride her again." He did and Nunsuch won, and the prince gave Tod a diamond pin and a set of his racing colors.

There were other of the prince's horses to ride, and other encounters. At one of these Edward said that although he was no gambler and hardly ever bet more than £25 on any horse, he would occasionally make an exception and "risk a couple of hundred on anything that I was riding and that I told him I thought would win." One day Sloan was on his way to mount his horse in the Newmarket paddock. The prince beckoned to him.

> "Sloan, what are you riding?"
> I told him Encombe.
> "Do you think you have a chance?"

Sloan replied that Encombe was a good thing. Lord Marcus Beresford (Lord William's brother) spoke up and said that Tod was wrong. Dundonald would beat Encombe.

"I listened, of course, but before I left to get in the saddle I turned to the Prince. 'Never you mind what Lord Marcus says, your Royal Highness. You can be a plunger here and have a bit on me.' "

The prince roared with laughter. And Tod delivered. Encombe beat Dundonald in a desperate driving finish.

Edward was amused and took no offense. Others were not amused in the least by what they thought to be Sloan's presumption, in this and in many other things. Newspapers took up the relationship between the prince and the jockey and made the most, and worst, of it. Tod supposedly made personal comments about the prince. Tod was raked over the coals for this and didn't help himself by trying to explain what he had actually said. Lord Marcus Beresford was severe about it. "You should never speak of him at all."[17] Sloan didn't understand the ground rules nearly as well as he thought he did. This was a trivial matter; more troubling incidents would arise.

There was never any blemish on Tod Sloan's rapt recollections of Edward, "that great, kind, big-hearted man." Naturally, their relationship was a matter of immense pride to Sloan. "I used to think to myself how pleased they would be at home and how they would ask me all about it, and what the American papers would say." Tod was sensitive to the charge that he might be betraying his national democratic birthright. "I can tell you that although I come from democratic America, there was a wonderful impression left on me by the great personal attraction of that royal gentleman." That Tod believed it a personal attraction meant that it went much deeper than the mere glitter of royal favor. It went to the dead center of his being. On the very first page of his memoirs Tod had suggested the fairy-tale quality of these adventures, how astonishing it was that "I would some day shine in the world I knew only from picture-books." Most of all, how amazing that "I should be shaken by the hand and talked with by the prince whose coloured picture was given to us by the local grocery store at Christmas." That fairy-tale prince towered above Tod in every respect, yet far from lording it over him or ignoring him, the prince had singled him out for recognition, treated him with genuine respect.

In a poignantly revealing metaphor Tod later remembered that the prince attracted him "as a magnetic crane in all its strength will pick up scrap iron." He had been lowly and now the prince "lifted me up and put me at my best with my own thoughts and made me hope to live up to *what I ought to have been but what I was not.*" There can have been few individuals who derived moral purpose from meeting Edward. Tod Sloan was one of them. But then this is a fairy tale, though a true one. The little boy never forgot the fatherly admonition: "What I ought to have been . . ." The worldly little man didn't deceive himself about "what I was not."[18]

Tod Sloan's racing achievements in Britain stood out with dazzling clarity. People admired his skill and praised his manner

and behavior. "Nothing pleases Englishmen better than abso-
lute success combined with honesty of purpose." And another
writer observed that "there was no suspicion of gallery riding
about him." Still another believed that he was "straight and un-
squarrable."[19] This is worth remembering in view of what happened later. The circumstances of his first appearance also added
to his appeal: a lone invader, a fresh face, a challenger who bucked
long odds with nothing to support him but his own talent.

When he returned for his second visit (the first was an individual foray), he was most definitely not alone. In addition to
other jockeys and respectable trainers who followed him, he was
at the center of a crowd of dubious characters—trainers, gamblers, hangers-on—who constituted the second American Invasion. He recognized clearly what was happening. "After I made
a few successes there was no end to the people who came up and
claimed me." Who was to say no to those who came along to bet
on his horses and win money, to be present as he spent his money
on those around him? A writer for a respectable American sporting paper had given precisely such advice. "If I were a few years
younger . . . I would beyond question accompany the American
jockey to England and stick to his mounts. Every one of those
who went over from this country . . . came back with bulging
pockets."[20]

From the point of view of the bettors that was all very well.
Sloan might have looked at it from the point of view of his interests, and not theirs. Should he have been in such intimate
association with gamblers? A young man who had lived for a considerable period of time with Pittsburgh Phil Smith was probably unlikely even to ask such a question. He was only doing what
he had always done—what everyone (more or less) had done.
But now he was doing it in a different country and culture, a
thing he failed to face up to even when, years later, he brought
up the subject in his memoirs. "Indeed [the gamblers] went by
the same ship and claimed me on board—that is to say, they lost

no time in striking up an acquaintance," he wrote. Even then, he evaded the issue. "I didn't own the ship, so I was in no way responsible for them."[21]

Tod Sloan would have done well to reflect on the observation of a British writer who, in the midst of a favorable account of Sloan's abilities as a jockey, sounded a note of warning. "When Sloan leaves our shores it will be amid a chorus of regrets from the bookmakers. The discrimination he exercised in choosing his times for winning and losing might have been inspired by a desire to make them as rich as himself."[22]

# ELEVEN

# YANKEE DOODLE

Yankee Doodle came to town
Riding on a pony

As the controversy and ridicule associated with the monkey seat died down, British racing fans and writers were generous in recognizing Tod Sloan's riding skills.

T    actful
O    riginal
D    aring

S    kilful
L    ucky
O    bservant
A    mbitious
N    erveless

("Tactful," of course, referred to his riding style, not to his personal behavior.) Stories and anecdotes spread quickly about him and the amazing things he could do on a horse. Fred Rickaby, a jockey of few words and of good judgment, when asked about Sloan's riding, replied, "If I were an owner I should not run a horse unless Sloan rode it." Nouveau Riche was a good horse but in his old age had become "cunning and sulky." "I shall pull up my stirrups and do a Tod Sloan on the old brute," the British jockey Sam Loates announced. But when Tod rode him he ran like a two-year-old and won going away. Said his trainer, "I think the old horse thought he had a devil on his back."[1]

But it wasn't the devil the British associated with Tod; it was the Yankee, in style, personality, and language. Often voluble, he could also be, when it suited him, the sly Yankee of few words. Two instances. How did he describe his riding style on a day of fierce winds? "Lying low." What was his response to English riders who continued to think his riding absurd? "I guess I hope that they will keep thinking so." He was American too in his willingness to try new things, in his indifference to tradition, in his individualism and bumptious self-assertiveness.

> Of Toddy Sloan now let us sing
> Whose praises through the country ring.
> Undoubtedly the jockey king,
> Proclaimed by everybody.
>
> Unrivalled he upon a horse,
> Possessed of spirit and resource.
> One always should expect of course
> Some spirit in a toddy.
>
> Although of jockeys there are lots,
> Experts like Cannon, Loates, and Watts,
> It's Sloan that every backer spots,
> From Sykes to Lord Tom Noddy.
>
> And if some unbelievers smile
> At what they call his monkey style,
> They've got their money all the while
> Upon the mounts of Toddy.

So backers cheer and bookies groan
As race by race is won by Sloan
On horses chestnut, bay or roan,
No matter if they're shoddy.

They may be broken-kneed or lame,
He wins upon them just the same,
So here's to health, and wealth and fame,
Of Yankee-Doodle Toddy![2]

This diminutive Yankee was determined to go his own way. Success didn't diminish this desire but rather seemed to have intensified it. He refused to accept the security of a contract employer; instead, he accepted "commitments," provided the fee offered was sufficient, but he wouldn't—with one notable exception—be tied down to one stable or owner. He spent extravagantly, which wasn't unusual for a jockey, and he bet and gambled to pay for his extravagances. Despite his chronic need for cash, however, he didn't ride just to make the most possible money. He accepted many fewer mounts than were offered him, many fewer than his rivals. He cost himself a lot of money by not charging for gallops or for traveling expenses. He rode when he pleased and when it suited him. This determination to be independent, to defer to no authority, won Tod great respect, and a place in popular slang. The Cockney expression "on your tod" meant to be on your own, with no need to account for your doings; in Cockney rhyming slang it was "on your own/Tod Sloane."

He was American in flouting some of the conventions of the British racing world. He behaved rudely to some people, the curious obverse of his own prickly sensitivity to condescension, bullying, or rudeness. His boorish behavior wasn't a challenge to the morality or immorality of racing culture, however; he all too uncritically accepted that world as he found it. He simply believed that his preeminence in his line of work entitled him to respect. He deferred to those in higher social positions but in turn expected deference. That his rudeness and deference existed side by side is made clear by his own comment: "I know I have been off-handed and I may in consequence have been thought rude by those who were really anxious to do me good and whom to know was an honor and privilege."[3]

He loved the fashionable life—expensive clothes, fine hotels, first-rate restaurants—and was happy to pay generously for them. He didn't care for the comradeship of his fellow jockeys, spent no time with them away from the race track. "I had no friends to speak of among jockeys." He never even had lunch or dinner with any other jockey, "in my own or in any other country." For their part, other jockeys respected his ability, copied his riding style, but didn't like him. One writer insisted that "every American jockey hated his guts, including his own brother Cash, and tried to foul him up every time they rode against him." Tod rarely praised other jockeys. Early on he admired Henry Griffin and in later years considered Lester Rieff the best rider of his time. Among his English contemporaries he praised Fred Rickaby, "a real demon when it comes to a long bout," but dismissed as overrated the popular Tom Loates, who didn't "belong on the same street" as his brother Sam.[4]

Often he gave "rough answers" to those who annoyed or contradicted him. Many racing officials didn't like him. His one significant suspension from the British turf—three weeks—was for disrespect to a starter. But it would be wrong to make too much of this particular challenge to authority; jockeys frequently were in trouble with starters. Starting was a notoriously messy affair, and starters were often ferociously criticized by fans, writers, jockeys, trainers, and owners. His aggressiveness at the start, his desire to get off fast, these were an important part of his riding tactics. Yet he never went out of his way to ingratiate himself with racing officials.

His belief in himself, his positive thinking about what he might do, impressed the British as very American. But British writers were quick to discern that this self-confidence (which to

The King of the Jockeys relaxing in regal fashion
after a day at the races. Keeneland Library.

many seemed simply arrogance) was actually an unstable element in his temperament. He had come so far on his own that
he could not help but think there was no limit to what he might
do; but he also knew how precarious and difficult that way had
been, so at times he was fatalistic and depressed. That the magic
of his riding depended a great deal on his frame of mind was revealed many times. George Lambton trained a beautiful little
mare, Altmark, who had maddened him with her inconsistency.
She was running worse and worse at one point, and Lambton de-

termined to have one last go with the horse, and employed Tod, already recognized as being good on "shifty" horses. When it became known that Tod would ride Altmark in her next race, she was made a hot favorite. Still, Lambton was uncertain about her chances, and his nerves were not helped by the fact that Sloan, who hated morning gallops, had never seen Altmark before the race.

When Tod came to the saddling paddock Lambton was disconcerted and disheartened to find that he was badly out of sorts with everything and everyone. Just then Altmark was led to the paddock, looking as beautiful as ever. "Sloan gave one look at her. In a moment, he was a changed man, exclaiming, 'Oh! I shall win.' " (This was all very well, and encouraging, but there was still the race to run.) Altmark, a high-strung and nervous creature, encountered trouble at the starting post. The other jockeys, "not particularly keen on Sloan winning," stalled all they could. There were nine false starts; three or four times Altmark ran nearly a furlong before Sloan could pull her up. They waited at the post for more than twenty-two minutes. Lambton was certain that his horse had lost her chance. Amazingly, Altmark remained cool through it all. "I saw Sloan lean over on her neck. He appeared to be whispering in her ear," "seemed to have hypnotized her." At last they were off. Altmark shot ahead like a rocket. "Nothing ever got near her again."[5]

Sloan exercised his magic in many ways. Through his hands: judgment of pace was crucial to his success, and "he had pace at his fingers' ends"; his touch was "exquisite." Through the power of his will: he drove Rosey O'More, a very ordinary horse, "into better form than she has heretofore ever shown." The power of his will could take cunning forms. Santoi, very stubborn and sour, fought him every stride of the way, so "every time I took a frantic tug at him I'd then let the reins slip through my hands as if I'd lost control, and Santoi would roar after those horses like a steam engine." Through his voice: "When Sloan en-

ters the paddock," a trainer said, "horses that he has ridden recognize his voice and turn to look at him."

Resourceful, adaptable, his Yankee magic also revealed itself in his ability to ride as the occasion—and the horse—required. There was an unforgettable demonstration of this in two
consecutive races. In the Jubilee Stakes he was up on Knight of
the Thistle, "a great big lumbering customer." Knowledgeable
horsemen were certain that Sloan was too little and too light to
handle him. As the horses went to the post he seemed "like a pea
on a drum." And sure enough, once the race was under way, all
Tod's persuasive efforts failed; his attempt to coax Knight of the
Thistle to race properly was futile. So Sloan resorted to the whip
"and slammed him home by a length."[6]

In the next race Tod was to ride Bobette, a two-year-old
filly. Bobette's trainer went to find Sloan, who was still recover-
ing from the previous race. "That was the meanest horse I've ever
ridden. I'm tired to death, and I can't ride any more." Tod lay
down on the grass, repeating, "It's no use; I can't ride. It's no use;
I can't ride." The trainer's frustration can be imagined. Just then
Bobette, a "little beauty," walked close by. Sloan, still lying on
the grass, asked, "Is that my horse?" "When I said yes, he was on
his feet in a moment, and all his depression and lassitude disappeared. He won the race easily."[7]

American racing writers were less forgiving, less amused by
such antics. In their accounts of Sloan's victories was a tone of
sneering deprecation. In May 1898 he won the Brooklyn Handicap on Ornament; he rode five winners that day and was deliri-
ously cheered by the crowd. According to relatively recent cus-
tom, the winning jockey was raised on to the shoulders of track
employees, carried to the judges' stand, and triumphantly de-
posited in a chair surrounded by a huge floral horseshoe. For
whatever reason, Tod refused to be part of this "time-honored
feature of Handicap Day." By anyone favorably disposed to Tod,
this might have been attributed to modesty, even if such mod-

esty was uncharacteristic. Instead, it was taken as evidence of the
"weazen-faced" Sloan's arrogance. He had blatantly revealed that
"offensive personality that makes him so generally unpopular
personally, in spite of his skill as a jockey."[8]

Tod's failures became parables of righteousness triumph-
ing over presumption. One writer reminded his readers of the
career of "honest Fred Taral," whose steadfast efforts had earned
him a "warm spot in the hearts of racegoers," at least until
"the Sloan craze attacked some of the racing crowd" and Taral's
image faded from the memory of many. However, one day at
Sheepshead Bay, Taral won a race, a "happy moment for the honest Dutchman," who glanced around "in triumph" at Sloan, who
had finished third. Note the "honest" Taral contrasted with the
brilliant high-flier, who was not singled out for his honesty.[9]

American writers could not make up their minds about
Yankee Doodle's success abroad. Some were on the alert for
any indication that success and popularity—especially with
women—were too much for him. In June 1898 "the small jockey
with a bad case of the 'big head'" was fined fifty dollars for being
impudent to the starter, "an indignity which the idol of the race
track soubrettes much resented as a limitation of the rights and
privileges which he should enjoy since his conquest of England."[10] But in countless newspaper reports, especially outside
New York City, the picture was of a hero in whom other Americans should take pride.

The response of the *Kansas City Star* is representative.
"TOD SLOAN LIONIZED," it reported of his English successes in
the fall of 1898. "The premier jockey not only of the new world,
but of the old," had "electrified English turf followers by riding
rings around their crack knights." Many of the stories about Tod
contained as much about his social success as about his riding.
"American Jockey Petted by the English Aristocracy" recounts
how titled women who belonged to the "Smart Racing Set" surrounded him in the weighing room after races—the Countess of
Dudley, the Duchess of Devonshire, Lady Curzon. "These

women, the cream of the aristocracy, shook Sloan's hand."
Through it all Tod remained "perfectly self-possessed and calmly
courteous." He was businesslike, regarding the attentions paid
to him as secondary to the business of winning races.[11] But secondary or not, Tod was continually and discreetly identified as a
man attractive to women—aristocrats and others—bearing out
the old race track adage that "those pygmies never go short in the
female stakes."

There was an American invasion of another kind as well.
Yankees, money, and the English aristocracy formed a familiar
chapter of Anglo-American social history in the 1890s, the high-
water mark of marriages between the children of American
plutocrats and the heirs of English titles. By the end of the nineteenth century one historian estimated that five hundred American women had married titled foreigners, taking $220 million
with them to Europe. The quest for titles is described in wonderful novels and stories by Henry James and Edith Wharton
and in popular stories, such as Mrs. Burton Harrison's *Anglo-
maniacs,* of 1890.

The first and most important of these matches was that of
Jennie Jerome, daughter of the New York sportsman, and of
Lord Randolph Churchill, in 1874. Their son was Winston
Churchill. The most magnificent match was that of Consuelo
Vanderbilt, daughter of Mr. and Mrs. William Kissam Vander-
bilt, of the Marble House, Newport, and of His Grace, Charles
Richard John, ninth Duke of Marlborough, of Blenheim Palace.
The wedding was the subject of enormous newspaper publicity
and the marriage the subject of much irreverent fun. A cartoon-
ist for *Life* magazine drew the duke as a ragged Columbus,
with the Vanderbilts meeting him on shore laden with wampum.
Finley Peter Dunne, a popular humorist, said through his Irish
plebian figure, Mr. Dooley: "Anyhow, it was arranged. 'Twas
horse and horse between thim. The Ganderbilks had th' money,
an' he was a jook." The marriage settlement included $2.5 mil-
lion in railroad stock and annual $100,000 payments for the re-

Tod Sloan and Jesse Lewisohn. Tod's story became a social chronicle as
well as a racing one. The Blood-Horse Publications.

habilitation of Blenheim and the building of Sutherland House,
in London, at a cost of $2.5 million. The match cost the Van-
derbilts $10 million, all told.[12]

So it was not surprising that the Tod Sloan story became a
social chronicle as well as a racing one. Although dramatically

contrasted with arranged marriages between aristocrats and plutocrats, it was a very old story in its own right: the struggle for
social position, the "nobody" pushing and scrambling up the
ladder. The appearance of this small, assertive Yankee Doodle
Dandy in a world of large, powerful, and eminent persons gen-
erated a stream of anecdotes that circulated by word of mouth
and by accounts in the popular press, the truth or falseness of
which was less important than the notoriety he sought, and
gained, in the glamorous world of fashion, theater parties, lavish dinners, and exclusive hotels.

Clothes made the little man. Like opera divas of the day or
the queens of the theater, he traveled with innumerable trunks
of clothes, changed his outfits several times a day, and took pride
in the elegance of his size three shoes. A London tailor devised a
short jacket with two buttons and a flyaway waistline (to com-
pensate for his stubby legs), which was known for a while as the
"Sloan swagger." There was a kind of innocent charm about such
vulgarity—"round about the Savoy certain people used to look
upon me as a curiosity"—but a very different sort of line was
crossed by the report that he had said to that most famous of
fancy dressers, the Prince of Wales: "Eddie, my boy, you look like
a fat bloody walrus in that bloody tailcoat you're wearing." Absurd, of course, given Tod's reverential attitude toward the
prince, but no doubt Tod said *something*.[13]

Then there were the other stories about Tod's encounters
with the rich and famous. There was the Belmont story. August
Belmont was supposed to have made a fuss about the cost of the
hotel suite he had booked, to which the manager retorted: "Oh,
no, sir, I assure you I am not asking too much, for Mr. Sloan is
paying more." There was the Monte Carlo story. Tod was supposedly commanded to appear at the casino to cut cards, for good
luck, for an "eminent person." He had the nerve to refuse to do
so, only to be informed that he had perhaps unwittingly crossed
another line. "You had better come, monsieur; it's the Grand
Duke Michael [Romanov]." There was the King Leopold of the

Belgians story, King Leopold who had so graciously "recognized Tod and spoken to him" at Trouville. As the story went, Tod had commanded the best table in a restaurant and, when asked to do so, refused to give it up to the king. "It was a stupid story to invent, but many people who did not like me began to repeat it, making me out what I really wasn't."[14]

But what was he, as represented by these stories? No doubt they portrayed him, for some, as a crude, insolent upstart. Yet for many British and American racing fans they must surely have had the opposite effect—of provoking admiration for his standing up to bullying snobs. No doubt this is one reason that the stories circulated and circulated and would not be put down. Tod Sloan, Yankee democrat. He was not the first. The extravagant behavior of jockeys, before and during Sloan's day, had always had about it suggestions of the resentment felt by those below for those above, even when it was partially concealed. Winnie O'Connor had understood this in describing his fellow jockeys "throwing our money around and drinking the bubbly and courting the pretty girls and never so much as tipping our hats to the millionaires and dukes and kings who hired us to ride for them."[15] Hired, not bought. But jockeys had to remember that it was the millionaires and the dukes who ran the best race courses, who established the rules of racing and had the power to enforce those rules.

Even in the greater social freedom of the 1890s, in the heyday of his money and fame, Tod Sloan knew, or should have remembered, that there were still rules ignored, lines crossed, at one's peril. Given this, the Ascot Incident was troubling. One evening after his day's work Tod, dressed conspicuously in a white yachting suit with white braid and a peaked white yachting cap, was dining at the race course restaurant. An unidentified person there apparently took exception to his presence or to his dress, or to both, and, it is said, gave money to a waiter to upset the table at which Tod was sitting. In the melee that followed Sloan fought back, striking the waiter with a champagne bottle;

in Tod's words, it was a "little jab, hitting him on the neck." There was some bleeding. Friends advised Tod to "square" the waiter by paying him £5. He did. Later, a blood-stained £5 note was returned to him with the message that the victim wasn't going to be bribed for the injury. Newspapers took up the story and transformed it. It became a murderous attack on an unoffending servant by an American roughneck. Much, naturally, was made of the £5 payment as evidence of a guilty conscience. Now he was the upstart Yankee, oppressor of the working class.

Lord William Beresford assigned a person to be always in Tod's company, a "big fellow," a "sort of minder" whose job was to "see me through any little incident which might arise." Lord William also paid the waiter several hundred pounds to hush the story up; instead it became exaggerated with each retelling. By chance, four years later, Tod overheard a policeman talking about the incident. "Wasn't I at Ascot when Sloan slung that magnum at the waiter and split his skull. Hot stuff I tell you. Yes, that there Sloan is mustard. What he don't know isn't worth picking up, but he can ride—I'll give him his due. He's a fire eater, that there Sloan."

Whatever happened that evening (the identity of the alleged instigator of the fracas was not established), Tod Sloan thought of himself as the victim. The world was always threatening, hostile. He had learned from Professor Talbot not to run away from a fight. "There had been one or two instances before when I had been hustled rather badly," he later wrote. But he insisted that he had learned to be "aggressive as little as possible, never getting into arguments unless there was a 'butt-in' on somebody else's part, which there frequently was." The Ascot Incident rankled for years. "I am not a giant," he commented, not ironically, "and didn't know exactly how far those two intended to go." How odd to be described as a bully and an aggressor. "It seems strange that such a small man as myself should have been the object of such antagonism."[16]

Yankee Doodle Tod was a portent of the immediate future.

The democratization of sport was both cause and effect of its becoming part of the capitalist world of popular entertainment. Jockeys had always been menials, available at their masters' whim. Now, unlike pugilists who began to make big money and gain widespread popularity but still were snubbed socially, jockeys were moving up the social ladder. Sloan was not the first jockey to attain personal celebrity. In England he had been preceded by the great Fred Archer (1857–86), the premier rider of the 1880s, who had achieved remarkable popularity. People blocked the street to see him leave his hotel; when he was married, a special train brought cheering supporters to Newmarket for the event. Archer, practically illiterate, was avaricious, unscrupulous, "and won some clever races."[17] He was also a tragic figure; his wife and child died, and he committed suicide on the anniversary of his wife's death. For the general public, he remained the model of the restrained and modest hero.

Tod Sloan was neither gentle nor modest; the deference in his makeup was proportional to his size. He didn't keep his place because he didn't wish to and because the location of his place was rapidly changing. "The American jockey to-day is monarch of all he surveys and thoroughly realizes and makes use of his power," morosely observed the *Spirit of the Times* in 1897. This outraged many people, and Tod Sloan became the focus of that anger. The outraged would have done well to have recalled the words of another small man, master of a very different line of work, the poet Alexander Pope: "A set of us have formed a society, who are sworn to *Dare to be Short,* and boldly beat out the dignity of littleness under the noses of those enormous engrossers of manhood, those hyperbolical monsters of the species, the tall fellows that over look us." A later writer understood the changed historical situation in which Tod Sloan expressed his own little man's defiance. "Those critics who complained about jockeys earning more than bishops probably never considered the relative odds of reaching the top doing God's work or assisting man's play."[18]

In our day, assisting man's play has become one of the most
lucrative ways of earning a living. Tod Sloan understood what
was happening and took full advantage of it. Masterful individuals competed for his services. William Whitney paid him hand-
somely to travel across the Atlantic to ride in one race, which
showed dramatically how the market winds were blowing. But
as a later historian wittily observed: that "skinny dwarfs were paid
better than the greatest statesmen of Europe" and of America,
and that "men as small in intellect as in stature" earned far more
than brainy professionals, was a novel situation a century ago and
caused great resentment. But if it is still resented in our time, it
is very familiar.[19] Where Tod Sloan led, Babe Ruth and Pelé and
Michael Jordan have followed.

# TWELVE

# TROUBLE

The American Invasion reached its climax in 1900. Several jockeys followed Sloan to England, and four of them—J. H. "Skeets" Martin, Danny Maher, and the Reiff brothers, Lester and Johnny—became very successful. Johnny Reiff, even smaller than Tod, "the merest child to look at," became a special favorite; he was a "real wonder" and possessed a Sloan-like sense of pace. The Reiffs were quickly in great demand and in 1900 had almost twelve hundred mounts between them. Danny Maher was overshadowed at the time but went on to an outstanding career in England; much respected, "skilful and Straight," he was sensationally successful in the Derby, winning it three out of four years— 1903, 1905, 1906.[1]

For a while, English riders feared that they might be crowded out entirely. The "monkey seat" gave way, as a descriptive phrase, to the "American seat," and by 1900, though a few unreconcilables still

grumbled about it—"I endorse the fervent regret that Columbus should ever have discovered America"—the prevailing view
was that English riders had been too slow in adopting the American style. "It looks as though they were very foolish in not
quickly realizing what has for some time been obvious to the general public, for if they were being defeated by a style of jockey-
ship and not by individual superiority, it is no discredit to them,
but the sooner they adopt that style the better." A few English
jockeys went further than their models; one so flattened himself
out on the horse's neck that he looked like a toboggan coming
down the run. "How very much amazed an old frequenter of
Newmarket would be if he were to return and watch the jockey-
ship now in vogue."[2]

Jockeys were the most obvious and controversial element
in the American Invasion, but trainers were important too. They
brought with them American methods, and these were a source
of some contention. The Americans were "as far as possible opposed to the notion that a horse is a machine"; training, they believed, should be adapted to the temperaments of individual
horses. American trainers, for example, looked on Newmarket
Heath as a kind of playground where their horses could get recre-
ation as well as work. Americans valued cleaner and airier stables.
They had for a long time emphasized the running time of a race
more than the British had; American race tracks were more
nearly uniform than were British courses, so time meant more as
a standard of comparison. American trainers judged a horse's
condition much more by time trials than did the British, and
they worked to instill a clocklike sense of pace in their riders.[3]
But none of this would account for the resentment the English
increasingly felt about the American invaders in general and
about American trainers' methods in particular.

The most disturbing source of that resentment was dope.
There seems to have been very little doping of horses by English
racing men, other than occasionally dosing with brandy or
sherry; anything else—cocaine, heroin, or laudanum, for exam-

ple—was little known. So rare was it, and so little imagined as a threat to the integrity of British racing, that there was no rule on the books of the Jockey Club prohibiting doping. It was assumed to be very bad for the health of the horse and of little help to performance. Anyway, it was supposed to be a thing not done by a true sportsman.

American trainers were widely known or believed to dope horses, some occasionally and discreetly, others pretty openly. The leading American trainer in England was Enoch Wishard. In 1899 he saddled fifty-four winning horses, more than any other trainer in the country. It was he who brought the Rieff brothers over and furthered their careers. In 1900 he lived with them. He was undoubtedly a shrewd trainer and bettor and supposedly won a great deal of money, mostly on lower-class animals. His greatest success was with a handsome chestnut horse named Royal Flush, who had repeatedly disappointed his English owner and taught him "what an uncertain thing a racehorse may be." Wishard bought Royal Flush, who promptly got better and better, winning the Hunt Cup at Ascot and the Stewards' Cup at Goodwood.

George Lambton, a distinguished English trainer, knew Wishard fairly well and thought him "somewhat of a genius with horses." There was no doubt in Lambton's mind that Wishard "supplemented his great skill as a trainer by making use of the dope." Lambton called it a pity that Wishard ever took to doping, for he "would have made a great name for himself without it." "Whether Royal Flush was helped by a dope of course I do not know," Lambton wrote, adding: "I had many a talk with him and found him a most agreeable man, but we never got on to this subject."

In 1902, Wishard granted an interview to a racing journalist. In it he said that he opposed the use of dope on the grounds of utility. "I have never found anything of that sort that did any good," he said, but he coolly and candidly admitted that "I have heard of lots of things, and tried, I think, all of them."

But only in the past, in America. Some American Jockey Clubs had rules prohibiting dope, which confirmed in English minds that it was a pervasive American practice. The use of dope accounted for what the British believed to be the startlingly inconsistent performance of American-trained and ridden horses; they doped them when they wished to win and then ran their horses without dope, "and ran them badly," when they didn't want to win. But allegations were not proof. And there was an odd air of unreality about the subject, since proof of doping would have carried no legal penalties. George Lambton believed that "it was not till about 1900 that [doping] really began to be a serious menace to horse-racing. Even then, although there were mysterious hints of its wonderful effects, few people knew much about it, or really believed in it." No charge of doping was ever leveled against Tod Sloan, but as the leading figure in the American Invasion, there was no doubt guilt by association.[4]

Gamblers—big-time American plungers—were also part of the invasion, and with them dozens of smaller fry. George Lambton recalled, "I hated it for it upset so many of my old theories and ideas." Also, the crowd that came over was a pretty tough one. Lambton remarked to an American racing man that he supposed "there were a good many rogues and thieves racing in America," and the American replied, 'There is not one, they have all come over here.' " There was Charles Dwyer, who had a reputation for very sharp practices. Tod had befriended him in 1898 and they spent a good deal of time together in California, not only at the race tracks but also hunting and shooting; and in that year they traveled together to England. Everything about Dwyer's gambling was exaggerated, winning and losing both; such accounts added to the hectic atmosphere surrounding the American contingent. Ed Corrigan, who brought over a stable of horses, was a California friend for whom Tod had ridden; with him came the irrepressible Riley Grannan. "At times Grannan was a perfect lunatic bettor," Tod commented. "Sometimes it came off." Bet-a-Million Gates, the epitome of the reckless spec-

A rare photograph of the wizard in action, in England, winning on
Knight of the Thistle.

ulator, came as well, frequently in the company of Enoch
Wishard.[5]

Jockeys, trainers, gamblers, all on intimate terms. Given
Tod Sloan's previous way of life there was nothing unusual in
this. He stayed in the same hotels with them and, as he put it,
"saw something of them, but not a great deal, for they were not
following me in particular but working out their own ideas."
These were not words to reassure the suspicious, who took for
granted that bad associates meant bad behavior. Stories about
money swirled around him, stories about his "fabulous winnings" on the New York Stock Exchange. (He was happy to describe himself rather coyly as a "lucky investor in Wall Street paper.") There were stories about the "very large sum of money" his
friends had supposedly won by betting on him, but others besides his friends had profited by his presence; so had the British
race courses. "The riding of the American jockey is still the all-
absorbing subject of discussion in the [British] racing world,"
one writer noted. "And there can be no question that the desire
to see Sloan has had a great deal to do with the increase in the financial returns of several of the recent meetings." Was there guilt
by association in that?[6]

In August 1899, while under suspension for "imperti-

nence" to a starter, Tod made a quick trip to the United States to
take care of business affairs, to dash up to Saratoga (where "he
made several bad investments at the roulette wheel"), and to buy
some American horses for an English racing man, whose name
he would not disclose. On his return to England he was accompanied by a new friend, Eddie Bald, a crack "outlaw" professional
bicyclist who had been suspended by American cycling authorities for various rule violations. Bald's presence was not by
chance. The wild atmosphere of speculation and rumor surrounding Sloan is best made clear by quoting a *New York Times*
story that sought, in a seemingly matter-of-fact tone, to explain
the conjunction of Tod Sloan and Eddie Bald.

> American turfmen believe that Sloan has a gigantic
> betting scheme on hand, and that Bald will be his
> commissioner or partner in the English betting inclo-
> sures. Bald, who has been somewhat of a plunger at
> the local racetracks this Summer, made a hurried trip
> to Buffalo before he sailed, and he is known to have
> taken considerable money to England with him. In
> England jockeys are not allowed to bet, but a good
> commissioner under the guidance of a shrewd judge
> like Sloan would be a menace to the peace of mind of
> the English bookmakers.[7]

And not only to the English bookmakers.

One long-standing aspect of the transatlantic relationship
was an American sensitivity to anything smacking of British
condescension and arrogance. Even so traditional a sporting
newspaper as the American *Spirit of the Times* came stoutly to the
defense of American horsemen. It angrily dismissed the charges
and insinuations as "old, moth-eaten, obsolete" anti-Americanism. The hue and cry about dope was an old story. "Good English horsemen," the *Spirit* insisted, "know better and understand the matter, the truth of which appears to lie in the question
of progressiveness." What this meant, apparently, was that in ad-

dition to devising the forward crouch, American trainers could also claim to have innovated methods of training and caring for horses. Finally, the *Spirit* argued that the criticism about gambling by the Americans was nothing more than the familiar anger of frustrated bettors and owners. "Utopia looms on the equine horizon, when all favorites shall win and never a bet be lost."[8]

The defenders of the Americans in England didn't need to mention Tod Sloan by name. He remained the premier figure in the field. His riding in 1900 was still masterful. But now he had more competition, not least from the other American jockeys, and the number of his wins declined. An English observer, in retrospect, argued that the most significant aspect of his riding was the increasing number of occasions in which he finished second; a number of these horses were "warm favorites," and the "natural inference" was that Sloan was "training off," by which was apparently meant that he was careless about finishing strongly (though the same writer admitted that finishing second might mean nothing of the sort). It was also charged that Sloan was riding much more carelessly; at Doncaster he "palpably fouled," though when summoned before the Stewards there was no reversing of the decision. (Sloan had won the race.) In any event, 1900 was by anyone else's standards still a very successful season; he raced 316 times and won on 71 of these, a winning percentage of 26 percent.

There were problems and troubles during the year, however, and many of them had to do with gambling. The most damaging was the Codoman affair. He received a telegram from Paris asking whether he would ride Codoman in the Prix du Conseil Municipal. He knew nothing of the horse, but a fee of £200 helped persuade him to go to Paris, where he met the owner, examined the horse, and insisted (against the advice of the French trainer) that American shoes be put on Codoman. "The plates made all the difference," Tod explained later, "and some people told me they had never seen Codoman travel as well before."

Travel he certainly did; though an outsider in the betting, he won the race comfortably. Tod's betting on the race was heavy and undisguised. "The race has been a good one for me and several of my friends"; the owner "picked up a big parcel of money over the event" and, in addition, gave Tod £700.[9]

Codoman was then entered in the Cambridgeshire, at Newmarket. Sloan insisted all along that he wanted to ride Berrill in the race, believing him the superior horse in the field; but another jockey secured Berrill. So Tod agreed to ride Codoman on condition that he be given supervision of him for the week before the race. There was great interest in the race and a tremendous amount of betting on it. "Sloan's faith in Codoman's ability resulted in the formation of one of the largest pools of the season." It became known that Sloan had accepted a gratuity—for purposes obviously unspecified—from an Australian named Frank Gardner, who had a large stable of horses at Newmarket and was betting heavily at the time. It was also well known—there was no attempt to conceal any of these dealings in the frenzied atmosphere—that Sloan and his friends were putting down a lot of money on Codoman. Tod later stated that he stood to win $350,000 if Codoman won.

Berrill won the race, handily, by four lengths, with Codoman second. The best horse had won. That no doubt didn't mollify the bettors who had put their money on Codoman to win, and they grew very bitter when word got out that much of the money bet on Codoman had been put on him to finish second. This was in keeping with Tod's private estimate of Berrill's superiority, but ordinary bettors knew nothing of that, and there was a pervasive sense that a betting coup had been pulled off by someone.

Sloan dismissed such talk. "The good thing hadn't come off, that's all." Even in his memoirs he continued to pooh-pooh the idea that there was anything out of the ordinary about the incident. "Well, there was the usual talk about my having done this, that and the other but apart from natural disappointment at not winning an important event, I looked upon it quite as an ordinary race." Yet he also added, "Looking back, I see plainly that there are plenty of things to blame myself for."[10]

No one else had this benign view of the proceedings. The Jockey Club held an inquiry and questioned Sloan. Certainly he had violated Jockey Club rules by accepting a present from a person other than the owner of the horse he rode. And he admitted to betting on the race, though only on the horse he was riding. The training arrangement, though informal, was a violation of the spirit of Jockey Club rules against combining roles as trainer and jockey. Apparently Sloan's explanation was satisfactory, however, because officially nothing came of the inquiry— at the time.

Nevertheless, this incident and others increased the sense that there were serious problems in British racing that the authorities were not confronting. In November 1900, at Liverpool, Richard Croker's horse Scotchman II, with Lester Reiff riding, defeated Lord Durham's Gerolstein after having been badly beaten by Gerolstein at Doncaster. The Liverpool stewards investigated, interviewing Reiff and Enoch Wishard, trainer of Scotchman II, and others. The stewards did not announce a decision in the case but referred it to the Jockey Club. At the same time, Tod Sloan was annoying people by campaigning sedulously to get a Newmarket license for Gardner; the plan apparently was that Sloan would become manager of Gardner's stable. This exacerbated resentment that reputable British trainers were being shunted aside by unscrupulous foreigners. Some racing people urged that Newmarket refuse to license any new trainers; others asked that British customs officials prevent American trainers and jockeys from entering the country, wild ideas indicative of the anger felt. Hard feelings were intensified by the sense that the flood of American money was undermining everything: "If it was not for the American owners, not all of whom are desirable acquisitions, [British racing] would be at a low ebb." As one writer graphically put it, "A stroll round Newmarket would show the bulk of the palatial establishments are in the hands of jockeys who never ride winners, and trainers whose favorites always get beaten; and yet with it all these two classes contrive to wax fat. 'How is it done?' is a frequent question, and rumor supplied many ominous answers to it."[11] Little of this touched Tod Sloan directly. He went on riding and winning; the money poured in and the betting public backed his horses and cheered him on.

And anyway, there were triumphs for Tod Sloan as well as troubles. Two events marked a summit in his racing achievement in the United States and in England.

In August he sailed back to America to ride William Whitney's Ballyhoo Bey in the Futurity at Sheepshead Bay, "the richest turf event of the year." He had been away from American racing for two years, and younger jockeys, all riding forward, were vying for the place he had vacated as the leading jockey. "The Return of Sloan," an editorial in the *Spirit of the Times,* suggested that he might be in for a shock. There was talk that his skills had eroded. But the *Spirit* hedged its bets. "Whether this is so or not remains to be seen; it is up to him to demonstrate whether he has lost his old time cunning and skill or not."

A partial answer came the day before the Futurity, when Sloan showed that "those who have any idea that he has fallen away in his marvellous skill had better discard it at once." Sloan, forced into a pocket, let his mount fall back without losing a stride until he got clear, and then, "entering the stretch[,] he rode the greatest whipping finish of the decade to win easily by two lengths at the last. It was an unexcelled piece of generalship."

The class of horses entered, the rivalry between their millionaire owners Whitney and Keene, and the return of the "one and only James Tod Sloan" combined to make that Futurity day "one of the greatest turf events of modern days." More than twenty-five thousand people turned out; the betting rings were a "perfect pandemonium." Sloan was an early arrival at the track,

This image, titled "The Gentleman Jockey," was
made at the time of Tod's celebrated dash back to
America to ride William Whitney's Ballyhoo Bey.
National Museum of Racing, Saratoga Springs,
New York.

attracting attention by walking up and down with a cigar "as big
as a policeman's night stick in his mouth," wearing a suite of
clothes "cut English," a straw hat with a flaring red and white
ribbon around it, patent leather shoes, and green and yellow
stockings.

" 'That's Sloan!' the wise-ones said."

"So he's the feller that hobnobs with the Prince of Wales,

dukes, lords and other great men, and also has a valet, eh? Well, I'll be blowed! He's got a fortune, too, they tell me."

Sloan rode in the race before the Futurity, and the outcome stunned his followers. When he came out of the paddock on his mount Jean Beraud there were cries of "Sloan! Sloan!" and "Good boy," and the band played "Yankee Doodle" in his honor. And then they were off, Jean Beraud wouldn't run a lick and Sloan "had to swallow dust by the pound." Perhaps he was disconcerted as well, because he seemed nervous in the interval before the Futurity and purposely avoided friends for the next half hour.

The favorite in the big race was a three-horse entry owned by James Keene, with odds of 4 to 5; Ballyhoo Bey was part of a two-horse Whitney entry, odds of 5 to 2. The other horses were all long shots. The money poured in: "Heedless of wilting collars and drenched underclothing, the mob fought and wrestled until the bookmakers were lucky to be alive." "The star jockey's downfall" in the previous race may have slightly reduced the money bet on the Whitney entry. When the horses came out to the paddock for the Futurity, Sloan didn't immediately mount Ballyhoo Bey but paced nervously, white in the face, rubbing his palms together, rubbing his chin with his right hand, looking vacantly into the distance. "He was thinking, perhaps, that he might be beaten, in which event it wouldn't be very nice to chronicle such a mishap when he got back to the princes and dukes." But if he won? "A smile flitted over the diminutive rider's face, and then it broadened into a laugh, which, however, was quickly suppressed, for the bugle was sounding."

After two breakaways and a delay of twenty minutes at the starting post, the field of twelve got off to an excellent start. The race was superb, a battle for mastery all the way. For more than half the distance there wasn't a length's difference between the five leaders—the two entries. Keene's Cap and Bells gamely made the pace; the contest "brought out every horse's good qualities and also tested the nerve of the jockeys to the breaking point." Sloan rode Ballyhoo Bey with consummate skill. "He rode far forward and kept his mount so steady on his feet that he did not lose a yard from swerving." Three-quarters of the way to the finish the other horses bunched together and seemed to pocket Ballyhoo Bey. This was no accident. Most spectators probably could not see this or didn't realize what was going on, but one sportswriter had no doubt about it: "The jockey boycott against Sloan was evident at every stage of this race." Winnie O'Connor, riding Tommy Atkins for Keene, later admitted that the "jockeys who stayed in America laid for their brother who had been abroad." "We were jealous of Tod Sloan. He had cleaned up at English races. So we homebodies got our heads together and decided to pocket the champion. 'We won't let that bighead win,' we declared secretly but earnestly."

For a moment, Ballyhoo Bey *was* blocked. Then Sloan saw a small opening, and as the field swung slightly wide, he brought Ballyhoo Bey down along the rail, "his foot almost crushed against the whitewashed fence, to push and bulldoze his way to the front," and made "a wild dash" for the finish line, closely pursued by Keene's Olympian. Sloan "worked both hands and feet with such effect that Mr. Whitney's colt simply walked away from the others in the last few jumps."

Whitney won $33,380. Sloan was paid $5,000 and all his expenses. Reflecting on this "memorable triumph," one writer contrasted the "little fellow, who ten years ago was just an ordinary stable boy knocking around looking for an odd job here and there," with the "great and only Tod Sloan [who] came, saw and conquered. He rode a grand race and is entitled to all he gets." For his part, Tod was as interested in spending as in getting. After the Futurity he went to Saratoga, where he rode Ballyhoo Bey again, and won again. Accompanied by two valets and ten trunks, he checked into a $125-a-night suite in the United States Hotel. Exulting in his success, he went to the casino and flashed a role of bills "as thick as his wrist," instructing Richard Canfield, the casino proprietor, that all his friends present that night were his guests.[12]

The second great event of 1900 was the culmination of the Tod Sloan fairy tale. He was informed by an intermediary (Lord Marcus Beresford) that the Prince of Wales wished to have first call on his services. Any jockey would be "proud of the distinction and privilege of wearing the royal colours," but for an American to be picked over English rivals was not just a compliment; for observers of the British racing scene it strongly suggested that the American presence would increase even more. "Many horse owners who have hitherto hesitated to desert the home talent will doubtless follow the royal lead." Tod accepted the offer "on the spot" and looked forward "with utmost pride" to keeping the contract.[13]

Back in England dark clouds were gathering. On October 10, at the Gimcrack dinner, an annual Jockey Club Affair, the Earl of Durham gave a speech on the condition of the English turf. Recently retired as senior steward of the Jockey Club, the earl was unsparing: racing was in the worst state it had been in for years. Newmarket had become a cosmopolitan dumping ground for touts, gamblers, and other disreputable types. Lord Durham had not been known to be hostile to American riders or trainers; two years earlier he had seen Tod Sloan as productive of good. But the brunt of his comments on that night was directed at the general influence of the Americans and the recent career of Sloan. He disapproved fervently of the methods of American jockeys and their followers, "who consider horse racing merely an instrument for high gambling." And he disapproved of Sloan's acting as rider, buyer, and trainer of horses, and of his meddling to enhance the influence of other Americans.[14]

The speech, much discussed in racing circles, could be taken as symptomatic of profound disquiet at the highest levels of English racing. A garbled version of it appeared some weeks

later in the American *Spirit of the Times,* which angrily dismissed
it as the sentiments of a coarse and anti-American backwoods
Tory. A poem, written by "Dutchman," one of the newspaper's
readers, satirized Lord Durham in those terms.

A Durham Bull

Lord Durham in the Jockey Club
Gave voice to private griefs
In terms of loud and long lament
'Gainst those bad boys, the Reiffs.

And sadly, too, he through his glass—
With anxious sigh and moan
Sees many a field spread-eagled by
That wicked lad, Tod Sloan.

His spleen he vents on Trainers, and
Berates the Yankee tricks
By which they get a thoroughbred
Into good winning fix.

Instead of grumbling like a lord,
And giving many a kick
Why don't their trainers and their jocks
Just learn to "do the trick"?

His Lordship's welcome to this hint:
We think he's got a "pull,"
Let him abandon racing nags
And breed the Durham bull.

The hint's well meant; he should succeed:
At least so it would strike one;
He has some point of that great breed—
How much he bellows like one!

Why does the Briton, Lord or Earl,
With colors furled retreating,

Cry Yankee trick and Yankee fraud
When given a sound beating?

One explanation we'll afford:
Turfman be he or cruiser,
Your British Earl and British lord
Is often a bad loser.[15]

Making fun of the earl was easy enough, but when the Jockey Club launched an investigation into his charges, it was clear that simple anti-Americanism was not the issue. A newspaper report explained that the Jockey Club investigation involved "graver issues, in which English, as well as American, jockeys and owners are concerned." Unable to dismiss the Jockey Club out of hand, the *Spirit of the Times* presented a different kind of evidence to substantiate the innocence of American jockeys and owners. Word had quickly spread throughout Anglo-American racing that the Prince of Wales had designated Sloan to ride. It was as if the newspaper had called upon Edward to testify for the defense.

> If any other proof were needed, but thank the stars it is not, it may be found in the action of the Prince of Wales engaging Sloan for next season. Putting aside his royalty, the Prince is a man of the people in the highest American sense of the word. He is democratic in his ideas, approachable, full of sound sense, a gentleman and a sportsman of the highest school. He is the very last man in the world to endorse anything illegitimate in the world of sport, and if there had been the faintest shadow of a truthful foundation for the Earl of Durham's hysterical invective, Sloan would never have been engaged to ride for him. On this point there is no room for the slightest hesitance. The boys are all right.[16]

But *were* the boys all right? As previously scheduled, Sloan was sailing for America in late November. It isn't clear what he knew, but he was certainly subdued, "melancholy and reticent but courteous." He said he dreaded the forthcoming interviews with American papers and added that "he regretted his 'American' following had made lots of trouble and that he wished he could break it up." He knew the ways of racing people, knew their suspicious, even paranoid nature. "There were plenty who were ready to say anything that could be suggested about horses who had run curiously well or unaccountably badly." But he found some solace in his clear conscience. "All the same, for jockeys who always rode to win, there could not be serious thought of any disaster." Lord Beresford had spoken to Tod before he sailed. Whatever he said may have accounted for Tod's gloom, which Tod later remembered in his memoirs: "Things look pretty black, little man, but we must hope for the best."[17]

# THIRTEEN

# JUDGMENT

The Tod Sloan fairy tale turned into a nightmare. On December 6, 1900, the Jockey Club, in its official organ, the *Racing Calendar,* published the results of its investigation into charges brought against Lester Reiff concerning an incident at Liverpool and against Tod Sloan concerning the Codoman affair at Newmarket. Reiff was "completely exonerated from blame," as were the others involved in the Liverpool affair. However, finding that the charges against Sloan had been proved, it "informed him that he need not apply for a license to ride" in the forthcoming year.[1]

Sloan learned of the decision from the New York newspapers, which carried a report of the action on December 7. Lord William Beresford's warning had prepared him for something, but he may not have anticipated anything so drastic. Questioned by a reporter just before his departure for Chicago and San Francisco, Sloan remarked with some annoyance that the Jockey Club "had plenty of time to inform me of the action they are said to have taken," but refused to discuss his plans, contenting himself with the optimistic comment that "I feel satisfied that there is some misunderstanding concerning the matter. Until the Jockey Club has sent me notification of what is intended I can say nothing about the reported action." History had caught up with Tod Sloan. He must have known of the immense authority of the Jockey Club. One writer, years later, explained Sloan's reckless disregard of consequences as a result of his being simply "stupid." But no one else ever described Sloan that way. Most likely he had simply come to believe that nothing like this could happen to him.[2]

It is not clear when, if ever, Sloan was "officially" informed of his banishment. Apparently the only record of the case in the Jockey Club records is the following entry in its Minutes Book for December 1900.

> It having been reported to the Stewards of the Jockey Club that Sloan had accepted the offer of a large present from Mr. F. Gardner in the event of Codoman winning the Cambridgeshire, and that he had betted on the race, they enquired into the case.
>
> Mr. Gardner, who was unaware of the regulation forbidding such presents, expressed his great regret at having transgressed it, and the Stewards, fully accepting his explanation fined him a nominal penalty of [£]25. They inflicted a similar fine on Mr. C. A. Mills, who acted as commissioner to Mr. Gardner, and finding both charges proved against Sloan, they informed him that he need not apply for a license to ride.[3]

It took some time for the full implications of the Jockey Club's actions to become clear. Tod Sloan wasn't "warned off," that is, banned from the turf. He was not specifically barred from riding in other countries; that of course was up to governing bodies in those other places. He wasn't prohibited from training horses in England or from managing a stable. And, strictly speaking, he wasn't denied a license as a jockey, only told that he need not apply for one. But in fact the Jockey Club had acted with crushing finality. All the things that Sloan still could do mattered little compared with the one thing he could not do, the one thing that was his career and his life: ride race horses.

The Jockey Club's decision, the "only subject of conversation" at all the London sporting clubs, was said to have come as a "total surprise to the racing world[,] as it did to [Sloan's] closest followers." There were reports and statements in newspapers about how Sloan would respond: that he would contest the decision and vindicate himself in England; that he would apply to various American tracks to test the efficacy of the English ban. His final position was to decline "to say anything regarding himself and English turf matters," and to refuse interviews. He was probably uncertain about where he stood beyond the forthcoming year, and he may have decided to wait to find out, through friends in England, what the future held and thus not further antagonize authorities. Tact and restraint on his part had come late and slowly, but perhaps it wasn't too late to mend fences.[4]

If Tod had hoped that the American public would be sympathetic and would rally to his side, he must have been quickly disappointed. One early newspaper had been supportive, suggesting that, because he hadn't been "ruled off" English race courses, a door remained open for a riding license in the United States and "subsequent reinstatement in England in days to come." And "thousands will welcome the fact." Most newspapers didn't take sides. Much of the public may have been sympathetic to him and seen the action as just another example of the arrogant high-handedness of the upper class. But such populist sentiments cut both ways. Winners are both admired and resented. When someone—especially such a small someone—raises himself above the common level there are many eager to see him tumble, as in the voice calling out at the time of Tod's victory in the Futurity: "Since Sloan has been travelling with Princes and Lords he has become stuck up."[5] And of course there are always those who assume that there must be important reasons for authorities to do as they do. Where there's Sloan, there's fire. When word got around that the Prince of Wales would not honor his commitment to Sloan as his jockey, it weakened Tod's general standing.

Nor is there reason to suppose that Tod wished to woo public opinion. If he had hoped that American racing notables would support him—some were men whose friendship he thought he had won and whose company he had enjoyed—he would have been disappointed. Their response didn't fit any pattern. Philip J. Dwyer, president of the Brooklyn Jockey Club, was not a member of the inner circle of racing magnates and, in terms of social class, might have been expected to sympathize with Sloan the underdog. But he was vehemently in support of the Jockey Club's decision, "a move which is for the best interests of the turf all over the world." If that was not emphatic enough, he added that Sloan "has been doing so many things his own way during the past year that he is generally regarded as a disturber." Dwyer gave no examples of what those disturbances had been; his condemnation may have been all the more persuasive in only hinting at the magnitude of Sloan's transgressions. William Whitney, with memories of Ballyhoo Bey freshly in mind, was generously sympathetic, calling Sloan the "greatest artist in his profession and honest. I fully believe that if Sloan made a mistake in a race it could be laid to over-eagerness and his overconfidence in his ability to win." Whitney added, candidly and surprisingly, that he didn't realize a jockey could be penalized for receiving a gratuity.[6]

Why did the Jockey Club act as it did? There is no question that Tod Sloan violated the rules. He admitted accepting money from Gardner and betting on the Codoman race. He knew that he was violating Jockey Club regulations, and pretending ignorance would have been no excuse. As a contemporary writer put it, "Going to ride in a foreign country, [Sloan's] first business was to acquaint himself with his surroundings and failing this, the midget has only himself to blame." At the same time, Gardner and Mills claimed ignorance and were given nominal penalties. It is obvious that the Jockey Club singled out Sloan for special punishment. The Codoman affair gave them the chance, and they threw the book at him.

There were several reasons for this. Sloan's preeminence made him an unavoidable target. British racing people were genuinely alarmed at the pervasiveness of the gambling, and at the huge amounts of money involved. It wasn't as if the heavy wagering on the Codoman race was an isolated instance; Sloan was blatant in his betting. And Sloan was more than just occasionally in the company of undesirables; he was the center of the company. There is no question that he came to symbolize what was most worrying about the American invasion. How could action be taken against anyone else without his being disciplined first?

There was something else involved as well—the pent-up resentment at his presumption, his brashness, his vulgarity. He had annoyed people from early on, but what now became apparent was that this annoyance had become deep resentment. The day after the notice in the *Racing Calendar*, one sporting journalist insisted that he didn't wish to exult over a man who was down but then proceeded to exult in uncompromising fashion. "Nobody denies that Sloan is a very fine horseman, but little else can be said in his favor." Further: "His manners are far from admirable, and he appears to regard himself as the equal, if not the superior, of his employers." The writer warmed to his work. "Sloan had for months past developed megalocephalic symptoms, which in plain words, means 'swelled head.' He had received so much attention that he began to think he was a necessity to the English turf." Another writer expressed relief that "This unseemly 'high-falutin' was nipped in the bud" and was pleased to see the uppity Yankee humbled. "In England a jockey is just a jockey. He has a definite place allotted to him in the social scale and is expected properly to fill it, with due deference to the powers that be as regards the surroundings of his profession. Sloan's democratic ideas ran away with him." It wasn't only in England that this phenomenon revealed itself. Phil Dwyer, in applauding the Jockey Club's decision, said, "Sloan has been lionized wherever he has gone, owing to the success he has had, until he received the idea that [he] was the one and only person on the earth."[7]

Once Tod Sloan was down it was difficult for anyone to regard him and his situation with any sympathy. He had strutted and boasted and showed off and done what he wanted, and who was there to see beyond that? But a later historian of English racing summed up Sloan's situation with understanding: "Young, brilliant, generous, extravagant, and candour compels the addition of the word 'vain,' Sloan found himself with a fortune in the bank after a couple of seasons' riding, and quickly became the mark of all the 'boys' on the Turf. He was surrounded by bad-hats and by pugilists and toughs of every description. He was made a tremendous fuss of by the female sex. . . . In a foreign country who was there to guide him, to give him a steadying word in season, to beg him to avoid this gang, to discountenance the advance of those sharps? Nobody." He had started out in life so much on his own, and he had come to crave companionship. Tod Sloan by himself had been a lonely way; Tod Sloan and his friends was a catastrophic one.[8]

He had brought to England the mores of the racing culture in America at their most common. It was a culture that showed no mercy or respect for the naive, so it is striking that Sloan had come to misunderstand the vulnerability of his position. He was a brash, little, talented outsider. He may never have realized how much he was on unfamiliar ground. *Tod Sloan by Himself* is evasive and ambiguous, claiming innocence but also seeking forgiveness—we are never told for what. He could write

Bet-a-Million Gates, the
greatest plunger of his day.
Tod Sloan said of him: "One
day he almost lived up to his
nickname; he was betting so
high that he might have lost a
million dollars. The
bookmakers saw to it that he
didn't. They didn't want him
to lose too much in one day."
Keeneland-Cook.

of his relationship to the dopers and gamblers all about him that "the Jockey Club may have become uneasy through the many innuendoes put about." In the circumstances, "uneasy" reveals a startling capacity for understatement. Yet he recognized that there were "also rans who got round me, scraped introductions, and then traded on the acquaintance and used me in every way to pull their stunts." Another comment was simply arrogant: "It was natural that the in-and-outer career of some of the gamblers should rather scandalise old-fashioned people in England." As if *only* the old fashioned had cause to be alarmed by what was going on.[9]

Anti-Americanism may have played a role in the story, especially in the upper social circles. On the other hand, it is remarkable that so many British racing people, and the great mass of the racing public, embraced a foreigner so enthusiastically. His brashness and assumption of social equality may well have been seen as typical American behavior, and lots of people may have liked him for that. It was primarily his behavior, not his nationality, that got him into trouble.

Why did the Jockey Club act *when* it did? His reception in the first two partial seasons of 1897 and 1898 provided no cause for alarm beyond the innovation of the monkey seat. It took time for Sloan's activities to seem detrimental to British racing. It took time to assess the full extent of the corrupting influences of the American Invasion. By the end of 1899, Sloan's first full season of English racing, the American gamblers had come over in full force and then the tide began to turn. The Earl of Durham is probably representative of this change of opinion. By 1900 the Jockey Club felt that it could not put off taking some action, and the reason for this was, in terms of Tod Sloan's life and career, rich in irony.

Insignificant as he was, Sloan was caught up in the machinery of state. The Prince of Wales's retaining his services for 1901 activated the machinery. Edward delighted in raffish individuals and was allowed considerable latitude in indulging his whims and desires, sexual and equestrian. But what was tolerable in an heir to the throne was intolerable in a reigning monarch. In the fall of 1900, Queen Victoria began to fail physically. (She died in January 1901.) There was little time left to extricate Edward from an awkward situation even if the prince, a formidably obstinate man, might not have seen it as awkward or have wished to be extricated from it. In any event, the Jockey Club would have been prepared to have its way, whatever Edward's wishes. There is no evidence to suggest that the (now) king would have opposed the Jockey Club's action. To believe that he would have done so would be to invest Tod Sloan's fairy tale of the prince and the jockey with significance when there was none. Edward, the horseman, recognized Sloan's skill and wanted his stable to be its beneficiary. He was, for his time, unusually sympathetic to Americans and picked an American jockey over English ones. He was polite to Tod, no doubt amused by him. But that was all. The social and cultural divide between the prince and the jockey was unbridgeable.

Was it a downfall or only a setback? Other jockeys had been disciplined, forgiven, and allowed back. After sufficient time had passed in expiation of his sins and follies, might Sloan be allowed to apply for a license? That was his view. "I believed that if I lived quietly it would be all right in the following year." (Imagine a quiet-living Tod Sloan!) One writer insisted that he would be reinstated if he conducted himself "discreetly" and applied himself to the "correction and reformation of his manners and excesses." (Imagine a discreet Tod Sloan!) Anyway, there wasn't anything else to do. He would wait and see, and hope. He was twenty-six.[10]

He lay awake nights trying to make realistic plans, but it was hard—impossible?—to know what was realistic. One thing that was tempting and certainly *un*realistic was to raise his hopes too high. This was especially difficult when so many "well meaning friends offered hope." One acquaintance, Lord Harewood, didn't offer hope. Instead, he asked, "Sloan, what do you want to bother about riding for?"[11] Did Lord Harewood know something he couldn't say openly? Perhaps he meant well; but asking Tod whether he wished to "bother about riding" was like asking whether life itself was a bother.

It was easy enough to talk about living quietly and discreetly, but it was a disheartening business, in London or Newmarket, having to explain to all sorts of people about what had happened. "I felt inclined to give rough answers, when strangers, especially Americans, became too inquisitive." It was sickening to know that he could ride as well as ever and then be advised, as Lord Harewood had done, to settle down as an owner. Anyway, that left out one crucial element: "The money to be made as a jockey was far in excess of anything possible to make with any stable." He tried to be honest with himself. "I was going through H-E-L-L."[12]

There was only one way out—to try new things for a while. He could afford to do that. He estimated that he had $300,000 in ready money, which would surely last a long time and go a long way. William Whitney apparently offered to put some of Tod's money into an annuity that would take care of him in his old age. "I can always make money," Tod replied in his inimitable way. "I don't need anything like that." He had worked hard since he was a boy, and he now realized that things were perhaps not so bad after all. "I had money and had an inclination toward a long holiday."[13]

So Tod Sloan began a new life, with new interests. The first one was the current craze: motorcars. Somehow he got the idea that he and a partner would take expensive European cars to America and use them as models in setting up a factory for the U.S. market. "It was a serious proposition, this automobile idea." Indeed it was. Having invested $100,000 in five cars, the partners were horrified on arrival in America to find that they would have to pay 45 percent duty on them. Then his partner was fined

$7,000 for undervaluing the cars—Tod paid the fine—after which one of the cars was wrecked in an accident. To add to their woes, Tod had some setbacks unconnected with automobiles. "I went racing and managed to lose thirty-one thousand in one day, and I also lost a packet at cards." The entire enterprise was a disaster. He was out of the automobile business in one month.[14]

A new life and new interests. Actually, there was an old interest. Sloan had always loved firearms. When he was ten he had been given a single-barreled muzzle-loader for hunting rabbits, squirrels, and birds; when he was thirteen he made a "great purchase," a tiny double-barreled breech-loader with which he trained his eye. He thought then that someday "something much greater could be done." Now he found that something: trap shooting. Of course in those far-off Indiana days he had known nothing about pigeon shooting, "never even having seen a picture of it."

In the winter of 1900, immediately after the Jockey Club decision, he had his first experience with "the traps." By 1903, with the automobile fiasco behind him, he felt confident enough to shoot competitively. At Monte Carlo he entered the Grand Prix du Casino and did well but finished out of the money. Failure galled him. A few weeks later he decided to enter the Grand Prix du Littoral, but there was a problem. By this time he was already hard up; he had no money for the entry fee, "nothing but jewelry." A friend lent him enough to pay the fee and to place a bet on himself, at 50 to 1. Killing thirteen birds out of thirteen, he won first prize, 10,000 francs and a "big gold metal."

It was grand, mixing with princes and counts and the rich again! And it was expensive. Trap shooting, in these circles, was enveloped in an atmosphere of money. All his trap shooting friends spent and bet heavily. As Tod noted ruefully of one friend, "I should like to have all the money which Charlie Hannam has lost over pigeon shooting in one way or the other." And there were so many ways! For instance, the expenses associated with winning that gold medal. His gun, bought in London's Bond

Tod Sloan at Longchamps.
Caricature by Sem.

Street, cost £200 (about $1,000). Then there were the other expenses, including 50 francs for the man who picked up the last bird Tod had shot. As always, there were ladies around, and two of them claimed the wings of that last pigeon, so each wing had to be mounted on a hat to suit its wearer. "That was a trifle," he said gallantly. The dinner Tod gave on the evening of his victory—with a bottle of Champagne to each person with each course—was not a trifle. The bill was 1,400 francs.[15]

A new life, but old habits. Besides shooting, there were "other bits of money" to be picked up in the casinos. Tod believed in the adage that "fortune never comes singlehanded," so when things were going well he believed in going all out. An instance was the good luck associated with winning the gold metal at Monte Carlo. After the entry fee and the bet on himself there were a few francs left over from the money the friend had loaned him. Tod went to the casino and, starting off with three straight roulette bets, was able to return to his hotel with 100,000 francs in his pockets. Sometimes good luck and bad luck were jammed together. At Dieppe he had a "wonderful experience" of this. In an hour and a half of baccarat he won 1,000 pounds; instead of quitting, he kept on and soon had lost that 1,000 pounds and the 700 he had had to start with. He got up from the table "feeling pretty sick" and went to have a drink. He had 7 francs in his pocket. One franc for the brandy, one he put aside for the cloakroom attendant. "I was determined to go home without a *sou,* so I put the remaining five-franc piece on the gambling table as I went out, intending to throw it away." But he won and won again and again, and in another hour he had cashed in 27,000 francs.[16]

The gambling habit that Tod couldn't control helps explain where the money had gone. And as well: "Nothing would do for me but the best suite in the hotel." And then there were those "others" to pay for—a valet, a chauffeur, and various servants. He fitfully understood his state of mind. "When we are gambling we do not pay much attention to a little matter like daily expenses." Nor was that all. Americans visiting Maxim's, in Paris, would have noticed a diminutive man, "smooth-faced, and in correct dinner clothes," seated at a big table and "surrounded by a dozen or more of the prettiest and smartest-dressed *coccotes,*" who were paying him the "courtesans' tribute to Success." That was Tod Sloan, "kinging it over a herd of Maxim harlots, the apotheosis of strut." At times, Tod *was* Mr. Toad.[17]

Other interests, other bad habits. In France Tod also bought and sold horses, and he gave advice about them, though "there was no money in that." Even so, "sticking to my own business— horses—was perhaps far and away the best thing to do." Or was it? In May 1903 he was involved in an incident with the Jockey Club of France. He had a financial interest in Rose de Mai, the second favorite, at 4 to 1, for the Prix de Diane, to be run at Chantilly on May 20. On the morning of the race, after exercising the horse, Tod let it be known that Rose de Mai was coughing and unlikely even to start. The odds shot up to 12 to 1. But

Rose de Mai did start, was "heavily backed," and won in fine style. This sequence of events produced an uproar. The horse's French trainer was fined, and Tod was expelled from French tracks for "spreading turf rumors."

Tod responded vigorously, hiring as his counsel the man who had defended Alfred Dreyfus years earlier, filing suit for $40,000 in damages against the Jockey Club, alleging that, as he was neither the trainer nor the jockey of Rose De Mai and was engaged solely in galloping the horse, he was outside the jurisdiction of the Jockey Club. Eventually a court ruled in his favor and required the Jockey Club to pay all costs. However, it awarded Tod no damages because, it held, he had not suffered any serious prejudice or hurt. *Au contraire,* this affair caused him irreparable harm, not only in France but also in England.[18]

Now there was nothing to keep him in Europe. "Not a word had been said about my not getting a license for the following year." The fervent hopes of the two previous years had now faded into the dimmer anticipation that perhaps the stewards "would not keep the bar up forever."[19] In 1904, Tod Sloan returned to the United States and tried to find a place in the theatrical world that had so attracted him when he first came to New York City a decade earlier, to make a new career in another form of popular entertainment, vaudeville.

# FOURTEEN

# THE WIZARD

Famous, and with friends and acquaintances who could help him out, he started at the top. George M. Cohan, already a commanding figure on Broadway, wrote a monologue for him, and Oscar Hammerstein booked him into a vaudeville act at the Victoria Theater, at $1,500 a week. "I necessarily had a certain amount of nervousness as to whether I should make good or not," he wrote of his first appearance; but he felt he had done pretty well and had got "a lot of laughs on account of Cohan's witty lines." Unfortunately, by the time Tod dictated his memoirs, he gave only a general recollection of the jokes. There were some stories about England, "not altogether to boost the country I had ridden in, little yarns about some of the antiquated customs of the old country," one of them that shopworn favorite about cricket, a game so slow that "a boy could grow whiskers before the match ended."

Closer to home were two yarns told against

himself. In one, Tod advised James Rowe, a well-known trainer, to bet on a horse that he was riding that day. Rowe refused. After all, a few days before, Rowe had bet on the same horse and lost a bundle of money. But Tod answered by saying that this time it would be different. "This time, *I* was putting five hundred on the horse." That brought the house down. In another story Tod told Snapper Garrison, the jockey, that he could go on stage and make $1,500 a week. "You only have to tell them what you did when you were riding." Garrison's reply: "Tell them what I *did*? Why I wouldn't do that for ten thousand a week."[1]

"It doesn't perhaps look so funny in cold print," Tod wrote later. "But I got across with it—again thanks to Mr. Cohan." And, of course, thanks to the fact that his audience understood very well the kind of things that went on at the track. The *New York Times,* reviewing Tod's performance, reported that the audience was receptive but noted that "there were innumerable moments when [Sloan] looked as if he would rather be astride a thoroughbred than be before an audience," a poignant understatement. There couldn't have been much of a theatrical career in making fun of his errors and misadventures. In any event, Tod soon lost interest and so ended his vaudeville career.[2]

In his search for something to do with himself there was one last brief racing interval, a desperate attempt to re-create his riding career. In the spring of 1905 a group of American race track owners calling themselves the American Turf Association seceded from the Western Jockey Club, previously the ruling body. The new group was a throwback to the anarchist mentality that had dominated racing throughout the nineteenth century; it was as if the 1890s, in all their wild unruliness, were being replayed. Representing tracks in Nashville, Lexington, Louisville, Kansas City, and New Orleans, the American Turf Association adopted racing dates and granted licenses to any jockeys and trainers it wished to employ, among them Tod Sloan. Ed Corrigan, the rogue racing man Tod had known in Chicago and San Francisco, offered him $10,000 to ride at his newly opened City Park track in New Orleans. The money was "not to be sneezed at," and as "I had natural confidence and I never put on flesh," it was tempting. Sloan hesitated, however, because he would be riding at a track that, if not exactly outlawed, was likely to be barred by the other American racing associations. Riding for Corrigan would reinforce his reputation as a renegade.

Tod hesitated but then agreed to do it. It turned out to be a disastrous venture—poor conditions, poor horses. "I had no heart at all in the work which was before me." But as he reflected on it later, what stuck in his mind was not the damage he did to his reputation but, cruelly and surprisingly, that the younger jockeys, all riding in the now standard forward seat, laughed at him. Though he was only thirty-one, he seemed to them to represent a bygone era. Tod won five races out of fourteen, but "that was no good to anyone and I gave it up."[3] As a jockey, he felt as exiled in America as in England.

He went back to New York and in 1907 made another theatrical connection. He married Julia Sanderson, an actress who appeared in musical comedies and was described as one of the most beautiful women on the American stage. Tod publicly announced his reformation, renouncing gambling forever. "The real happiness which followed was the best solace possible for disappointments, and all those pleasant days, months and years helped me think that after all there was a great deal left in life."[4]

So he tried yet another line of work. He and John J. McGraw, manager of the New York baseball Giants, opened an elaborate billiard parlor at Broadway and Forty-Second Street, surpassing in opulence anything of its kind in the world, or so the proprietors insisted. Nevertheless, the billiard parlor failed. From this point on, Tod's efforts to live the high life became a series of dodges and improvisations. At the time of his banishment by the Jockey Club he was reputed to have had half a million dollars in the bank. That figure, like so many stories about him, was probably much exaggerated. But whatever he had saved, Tod had by this time succeeded in running through most of it. Pittsburgh

Phil Smith had lent Tod money, but that was lost with all the rest. By the time the billiard parlor opened we get a glimpse of how far he had fallen. Tod was sued by an architect for work on a house at Sheepshead Bay that Tod had bought, lavished money on, and then abandoned; in response to the architect's suit Tod testified that he was living at the Hotel Spalding, paying $90 a month for two rooms, and earning $50 a week at the billiard parlor.[5]

Gambling had always been an important part of his riding career. Now it *was* his career, despite periodic vows to give it up. In his memoirs, he recounted about his adventures as a bookie, telling stories ostensibly light-hearted in tone but with a sordid and despairing undercurrent. All he needed to conduct his business was an apartment with a telephone. Customers—"a pretty collection of all nations: grafters, diamond merchants, the knock-outs from the Balkan provinces and others"—flocked to his place. He noticed the condition of the carpets and chairs after his customers had gone: "The collection of cigar stubs and remnants of bad words took some time sweeping up." He was more or less back where he had begun as a little boy—sweeping up.[6]

"The show went on" until a New York state senator tipped him off that the police were going to raid his operation. "They came, looked around, went away. But bookmaking at that place was finished for good and all." So he moved to another site, an uptown hotel. It hadn't been going for an hour when the cops came, "smashed the door in and caught us all red handed." Tod somehow convinced the police inspector that it would be a terrible blow—"I had applied for a racing license, which I hoped to get"—if he were arrested and the newspapers found out. The inspector let him go. "That was the end of the bookmaking business."[7]

Maybe so. But he always was trying something—he had to try something. During his days on the fringes of theatrical culture he had encountered many sportsmen and men about Broadway, among them the remarkable Wilson Mizner, theatrical pro-

Tod Sloan at Nice, 1913. "I was only a jockey and now am an ex-jockey, a would-be trainer, a would-be at many things."

ducer, gambler, con man—one of those men who was in on everything without actually doing any one thing. Mizner, who had just lost money on a scheme to sell reproductions of Old Master paintings, had an inspiration in 1913. He would form a racing tipster service in collaboration with Tod. The name of the "disbarred demigod of the turf" was still something to cash in on, Mizner recognized; and what would give Sloan prestige as a racing tout was precisely "the fact that he had been ruled off the turf on a charge of complicity in a betting ring." Though he was out of racing, he still could pass as an insider. And sure enough "the bad reputations of Sloan and Mizner caused a rush to buy their tips." But after three days in which they failed to pick a single winner, the business collapsed.[8]

Sloan had never given up hope of riding in England again, though it was becoming clear to everyone but himself that his banishment from riding was for life. As late as 1908 the *New York Times* reported that Sloan had applied for a renewal of his license, and the probability was that it would be granted. "A strong feeling has manifested itself," according to a supposedly trustworthy source, "that Sloan had been sufficiently punished and that it is un-English to pursue him longer as an outcast from the English race track." It was believed that "even King Edward is interesting himself in the brilliant jockey."[9] Nothing came of this. Nothing ever came of anything. So he continued to move from place to place, from amusement to amusement, from failure to failure.

His marriage unraveled, the result no doubt of his drinking and gambling. Tod spent more time in England again, and it was in connection with this that he hinted at other marital problems, probably other women, for he later wrote that "much to [my] regret," Julia visited him twice in London. They were divorced in 1913.[10]

And then came his final encounter with law and authority in England. On November 6, 1915, Tod Sloan and a French woman companion were charged with maintaining a gambling house in London. Under the wartime Defense of the Realm Act, a hearing was held; in the Home Office records Sloan is listed under the heading "reported him as dangerous." On November 23 he was arrested on a deportation order and informed that he was immediately being sent back to the United States; his companion was deported to France. "When you hear the facts you will find I have been very unjustly persecuted," he told reporters as he was sailing, and added, pathetically, "I may return to racing in America." No other facts were revealed by Tod or by anyone else, but since he had been gambling and making book for a decade or more, there is little reason to suppose that he hadn't been operating a gambling enterprise, as charged. That he was deemed "dangerous" was attributable to the feverish wartime atmosphere in England in 1915. If he was dangerous, it was mostly to himself.[11]

Tod Sloan never returned to England, never again saw the "one and only great race course in the world," Newmarket. "Nothing ever laid out or adapted from nature ever approached it. Every distance, plenty of room, splendid going in all seasons—what can equal it?" His own words serve as the most appropriate epilogue to his English racing career. "It is a shame that I should leave in this way."[12]

Even as Tod Sloan, trapped in the agonizing futility of a nonracing life—"that I should go through life without the [second] chance I have prayed and longed for seems too terrible"[13]—spiraled downward into obscurity, racing writers on both sides of the Atlantic began giving him a new kind of existence, a life in history, a reconsideration of what he had done more than a recollection of who he had been, a reconsideration that is still going on.

One thing emerged clearly: the Wizard of the West had been a riding genius if anyone involved in so modest an activity as riding could deserve that much abused and overused term. But what sort of genius? There were differences of opinion about the answer to that question.

One school of thought emphasized riding talents that went beyond the monkey seat, talents more important than his style of riding. Believing that "jockeys are born and seldom made," the English trainer Richard Marsh, while not denigrating the importance of the new kind of riding, argued that "the genius of Sloan had nothing to do" with his style of riding. "He would have been just as great," March insisted, "if he had been taught to ride in the English style. He was full of brains and a vitality which he shared with the horses he rode." Harding Cox, an English sportsman and rider, also put himself in this camp—and enrolled Sloan as well. He recalled Tod "discoursing sweetly" on the subject one day at Monte Carlo. "Say, I figure that this seat has considerable advantage; but it's no cinch for any guy or dud jockey that takes a hand." The remainder of Cox's recollection reads ironically for us. "Believe me, sir, there's nothing to it unless you have the whole bunch of tricks up your sleeve."[14]

The prevailing evaluation of Tod Sloan's achievement since the 1920s does not dispute these skills but emphasizes that the new style of riding had historical and institutional consequences far beyond the realm of individual talent. Sloan's claim to importance (and all observers recognized the claim) was part of the impetus it gave to modern horse racing. The word that appeared over and over, one not usually associated with this jockey or any other, was "revolutionary." Sidney Galtrey, racing correspondent for the English *Daily Telegraph,* characterized Sloan as an "agent of change," a "relentless revolutionary." Although too young to have seen Sloan ride, Galtrey imagined the sight of "the amazing Tod Sloan crouched half-way up a horse's neck, whispering to it, setting the pace with uncanny judgment, riding as if inspired." Richard Marsh saw this side of the argument as well. "This change in jockey-ship has been the most revolutionary thing on the Turf that I can point to during fifty-odd years of association with it." Another writer summed it up: "It is impossible to gauge our debt to this American; safely may it be said that he revolutionised race-riding." The American racing journalist Joe Palmer made the case for Tod's historical importance in a tone of playful national pride. Tod Sloan, having forced jockeys "to quit making boat sails of themselves," achieved the unprecedented feat of making the English concede that "something they had been doing for two hundred years" had to be changed. "Sloan and the barons at Runnymede are really the only ones to do it."[15]

In retrospect, even the American Invasion had come to be seen as an instrument for change and therefore a positive development. The genuine English fears about doping and unrestrained gambling had galvanized the Jockey Club to initiate reforms. The presence of American jockeys and trainers also provoked a response that was eventually salutary for English racing. "There is not the slightest doubt that the coming of the Americans did us a lot of good and roused us from that feeling of superiority and complacency which is fatal to progress."[16]

Surprisingly, the reconsideration of Tod Sloan's career and riding accomplishments has focused little attention on the Jockey Club's decision to banish him. In one way, this is understandable. He admitted to violating certain racing rules. The members of the Jockey Club might well have believed that details didn't really matter; Tod Sloan was part of a disreputable crowd and was surely guilty of something.

And yet, there *is* more to be said. Of the two charges brought against him, accepting a gratuity from a third party was a relatively trivial offense. As a keen student of the turf explained, "If not actually winked at by the authorities, it was certainly more honored in the breach than in the observance by contemporary jockeys."[17] The main issue was Tod's betting, and in that respect the sentence, initially ambiguous, turned out to be excessive, for he was not given a second chance. To argue for some leniency on behalf of Tod Sloan is not special pleading for one individual.

In England, at the very time of Sloan's barring, there was a precedent for the exercise of mercy. Lord Durham, of the Jockey Club, at the 1887 Gimcrack Dinner referred indirectly to what was common knowledge—that the jockey Charles Wood was "pulling" some of his horses with the knowledge of the horses' owner, Sir George Chetwynd, who was also a member of the Jockey Club. Chetwynd sued for libel, and the case was referred to the Jockey Club because the "nature of the dispute necessitated a knowledge of racing on the part of the jurors." Lord Durham's allegations were not proved. Chetwynd won his case, but only a farthing (less than a penny) in damages was awarded him, making clear that he had behaved wrongly, even though the charges could not be proved. He resigned from the Jockey Club. Wood was refused a license. But there were persistent attempts to get Wood reinstated, and eventually, in 1897—the year Tod Sloan first raced in England—Wood was allowed to ride. He had "learned his lesson and bec[o]me a successful and honest jockey." And there were other such cases. Great pressure was often exerted by jockeys' employers, usually men of great position and power who didn't want to lose their services. A fair-minded authority has commented that "generally minor figures were cast permanently into the wilderness, whereas all too frequently those with influence or influential friends found their way back."[18] After a year or two, or five or even ten, as in Wood's case, why was there no second chance for Tod Sloan? Perhaps efforts were made; there were persistent stories, as we've seen, that this was so. Perhaps Tod's friends were less loyal (not for the first time) and less influential than he had thought them to be. Perhaps his being a foreigner made a difference after all. Perhaps, most of all, the manner and behavior of the impertinent little man made people wish not just to penalize him severely but to crush him once and for all.

The procedures of the Jockey Club must now strike us as fantastically arbitrary. Its hearings were private. Individuals—

many with very little education—were summoned before it and afforded no legal counsel. There was no formal basis for appeal. Apparently there was little formal recordkeeping. That the racing world of the later twentieth century would not tolerate such procedures again provokes the inescapable irony associated with Tod Sloan's life and career. He had no interest whatsoever in politics, and in temperament and attitude he certainly was not on the side of the reformers of his day. But a great deal of his importance has to do with what one might characterize as his role as inadvertent reformer. In England it was reform in riding and training, which led to a progressive improvement of the old tradition. But in America, while the new riding style was adopted everywhere, Tod Sloan represented for many everything that was wrong with racing culture as a whole.

In the United States, between 1900 and 1914, the continuing abuses and blatant corruption associated with racing provoked widespread determination to abolish the entire system, not to reform it. The racing life in which Tod achieved his fame was anathema to two powerful movements of the time, one essentially political, Progressivism, and the other essentially cultural, Prohibitionism. What brought these disparate movements together?

In its various local, state, and national versions, Progressivism aimed to restore civic virtue by regulating the excesses of big business and by uprooting political corruption in the cities. The most notorious instances of corruption were the big-city political machines, and the alliances between bookmaking syndicates and these machines helped to feed this corruption. Even when honestly conducted, gambling seemed a wasteful activity, distasteful to that aspect of the progressive mind which prized efficiency. On both counts, horse racing, though distant from the interests or concerns of most reformers, came into conflict with rationalizing modernism. So did the Prohibition movement. Though not directly concerned with horse racing, it looked upon the sport as unrepentantly associated with dissolute behavior, steeped in an atmosphere of immorality and lewdness.

Some reformers wished to prohibit horse racing of any sort, but most reformers concentrated on the gambling sites associated with horse race betting—city casinos and pool rooms. Under intense political pressure the Western Union Telegraph Company cut off its wire service to the pool rooms, depriving them of the information necessary for betting on horses; persistent police campaigns were launched to drive bookmakers into some other line of work. In fact, they were not driven out of work but were simply driven underground.

Next came the direct assault on race track betting. Legislatures in many states, including California, Illinois, and New York, made it illegal. Those who had always believed that horse racing wasn't a sport but only a means of gambling, pointed gleefully to the immediate decline in attendance and purses and to the fact that many American horsemen moved their stables to Canada or retired from the business. The U.S. Congress did its small part by prohibiting horse racing in the District of Columbia; the South, the cradle of American horse racing, went "dry" and antigambling at the same time. By 1912 only six states— Kentucky, Utah, Maryland, Montana, Oklahoma, and Virginia—permitted betting at race tracks. The rejection of the old horse racing order was as complete as it was swift. As a national sport and as a large-scale urban amusement, racing seemed about to come to an end.

And then horse racing made a comeback. Reform stalled and then turned back the forces of abolition. Out of this period of travail emerged an industry much better adapted to the urban commercial culture of the 1910s and 1920s, and horse racing once again flourished. While Tod Sloan, the ex-jockey, could only sit in the grandstand and watch, new attitudes and innovations associated with the riding style that he had introduced swept all before them.

The style and spirit of twentieth-century American horse racing was speed. In itself this wasn't new; the motto of the venerable American sporting newspaper *Spirit of the Times* had been "THE SPIRIT OF THE TIME SHALL TEACH ME SPEED." But now every aspect of racing was speeded up, mechanized, regularized. Sloan's forward crouch was a key element. His riding had been an all-out effort from first to last: speed and more speed. Short races became the rule; any race over a mile and a quarter was exceptional on American tracks. Horses were valued more for speed rather than endurance, and timing horses, which Americans had emphasized far more than the British, became the principal measure of quality.

Technological improvements, obstinately opposed in the

Belmont Park in the late twentieth century. Racing reached a level of affluence and organization unimaginable in the days when Tod Sloan began riding. Photo by Bob Coglianese.

1890s, became an important part of speeding up the rhythm and organization of horse racing. The Australian starting gate, in an electrically operated American version, did away with the frustrating delays and guaranteed a much fairer start. Trainers quickly trained their horses to adapt to it. The photo finish camera did away with subjective judgments at the finish line, doing for the ends of races what the starting gate had done for the beginnings: guarantee honesty.

These changes and reforms allowed races to be scheduled with precision; seven, eight, or even nine races could be run in one afternoon, adding to the appeal of racing for the vast number of urban customers and multiplying the opportunities for betting: more races, more betting, more revenue, larger purses. Horse racing increasingly reflected the ordered regularity of mass production in industrial America.

Another reform was a crucial element in saving horse racing: the pari-mutuel system, adopted everywhere. Betting became impersonal but also speedier and simpler: "All men are equal before the totalisator." Even more than efficiency, however, the pari-mutuel system represented honesty. As the bookmakers disappeared, the atmosphere at race tracks became more restrained and ordered. Legalized betting of this sort removed much of the taint from twentieth-century horse racing. And tracks of course supported efforts to squelch off-track betting, for their new gambling monopoly was an arrangement far beyond the dreams of any race track proprietor in the days of Leonard Jerome and the Dwyer brothers. In fact, a gambling subculture away from the track continued to exist; the pool hall was replaced by the bookie joint, with payoffs to the police, but the race track was curiously insulated from that set of problems. Tod Sloan's bookmaking adventures in New York City were characteristic of the new order. The betting monopoly that race tracks now enjoyed—lotteries and casinos having been abolished—made horse racing the greatest gambling enterprise in the country. Attendance improved, and growth in the number and size of purses and stakes instigated a rise in the number of thoroughbreds available to fill the increased number of races. The track's monopoly provided the revenue for cities and states, which took a fixed percentage of the money bet with machines. This municipal benefit was an important argument for legalizing racing during the Depression of the 1930s.

The assumption by the tracks, and to a considerable extent by local and state governments, of responsibility for honest racing meant that tracks had to develop a system of surveillance and policing to control cheating. Jockeys were now closely watched, as were, to a lesser extent, trainers and stable boys; secret police agencies supervised on- and off-track behavior. Stringent tests were developed to determine whether horses had been doped. Central racing authorities established rules and regulations. August Belmont and James R. Keene would have been astonished at the power vested in racing organizations, power equivalent to that of the Jockey Club in England. In turn, jockeys organized the Jockey Guild to protect their interests. There was no such body, of course, to protect Tod Sloan's interests, whatever they might have been.

In spite of these reforms, nothing can entirely dispel the ambiguities inherent in horse racing. For example, in May 1995 the Irish jockey Kieren Fallon, the leading rider in English racing, who had been frequently disciplined by racing authorities for violating the rules, was accused by a newspaper of deliberately failing to win a race at Newmarket. Evidence? Fallon won the important Chester Cup only twenty-three days after losing on the same horse at Newmarket. His riding at Newmarket *had* been erratic. And a trainer, who had been a supporter of Fallon's, said frankly that Fallon had ridden one of his horses very badly. Since then, however, other jockeys have not won with the same horse that lost at Newmarket. So what did Fallon's loss prove?

Fallon sued the newspaper for libel—and won; the jury awarded him substantial damages. Though apparently very unlike Tod Sloan in temperament and manner—no flamboyance, no desire for public attention—the parallels and contrasts between their historic situations are thought provoking. What if Sloan had been able to sue the Jockey Club and gain a civil trial? What if . . . ? But of course Sloan lived in another time and another world. A comment of Fallon's is resonant with the freckled nature of our lives in whatever time and historic situation we live; his is Sloan-like in its truthfulness and its ambiguity. Asked if he was an honest person, Fallon replied: "Most of the time."[19]

There is no law to keep an individual from associating with undesirable people, no law to guarantee prudence and good sense; but blatant examples of keeping bad company and of behaving imprudently now lead to severe punishment for jockeys, and they know this. None of this means that the moral millennium has arrived. Race tracks are not yet places noteworthy for their virtue. The naive and the gullible are well advised to shun them. Racing reforms have not abolished the essential ambiguities and imponderable aspects of the sport, nor has the parimutuel system abolished the odds against winning. Horse players still die broke.

# FIFTEEN

# STORIES

S tories. Tod Sloan's career, bordering on the fabulous, the nobody who became somebody, provoked stories: stories about his riding and his manners (or lack of them), about his outrageous comments and the money (exaggerated) he made and lost. His life illustrated the idea of the German novelist Herman Hesse that, however much one strove for objectivity, historical narratives remained literature. "History's third dimension is always fiction."[1]

In 1903, George M. Cohan read a newspaper story about Tod Sloan, a glowing estimate of his talent and a sympathetic account of his English misadventures. Cohan, a twenty-six-year-old composer and writer, was looking for a subject for a new musical play. He had gained a degree of recognition as one-quarter of the Four Cohans, appearing in vaudeville with his father, mother, and sister; and had written the music, story, and lyrics of two musicals, *The*

*Governor's Son* and *Running for Office*. Both had successful national tours, but neither was a hit on Broadway, and Cohan was
smarting at his relative failure. Furthermore, both shows were expanded versions of vaudeville sketches that he had written some
years before, extensions of the kind of roles he had been playing
for years. Now he aspired to something fresh and contemporary.

The story of the little riding man appealed to him. The role
was ideal for the five-foot, six-inch, 135-pound Cohan; and the
rhythm of horses racing paralleled the bursts of speed for which
Cohan musical plays were coming to be known. Even more, the
notion of Tod Sloan as victim of English mistreatment roused
Cohan's sympathy. Sloan's story was a parable about how ordinary folks are taken advantage of by those in power and in positions of social superiority. It would be a populist drama—Tod
Sloan, an American Everyman, and so the title, *Little Johnny
Jones*.

Cohan hoped, of course, that the show would appeal to the
sporting theatrical audience. His knowledge of the sporting part
of it came mostly from his business partner, a sporting theatrical
man named Sam Harris, a New York Jewish boy who went to
work when he was eleven, sold newspapers and became a salesman for a cough drop business, singing songs to attract customers. That was the only musical or theatrical talent Harris ever
revealed, yet he yearned to be in the theater. Fortunately, he possessed an uncanny sense of what people would pay money to
watch on Broadway or in the prize ring or at the race track. He
had once owned fourteen horses and had made a good deal of
money but had lost it all just before joining Cohan.

In those days no bank would lend money for a theatrical
production. Sportsmen and gamblers often invested in shows,
and showmen occasionally got involved with sports teams,
sometimes with disastrous consequences. Harry Frazee, a Boston theatrical producer, lost so much money on his shows that
he had to sell the star of his Red Sox baseball team. So Babe
Ruth became a New York Yankee. Eventually Cohan and Harris

found a Philadelphia sporting man who backed them. Cohan then moved into a hotel and wrote the book and composed the music in ten days.² *Little Johnny Jones* opened on Broadway in October 1904.

The first scene of Act 1 is set in London, at the Cecil Hotel, on the day of the Derby. Johnny Jones, the world's greatest jockey, is to ride Yankee Doodle. The hotel is overrun with squealing young women feverishly seeking to catch a glimpse of Johnny, who has other things on his mind. Weeks before, at the race track in San Francisco, he had caught sight of a girl, Goldie

George M. Cohan as Little Johnny Jones,
1904. Harry Ransom Humanities Research
Center, University of Texas at Austin.

Gates, and fallen in love with her; Goldie, who was attending a convent school but had somehow managed to get to the track, experienced an equally rapturous glimpse of Johnny. But money and class complicate the romance. Goldie is a fabulously rich copper heiress; her wealthy and snobbish aunt and guardian, Mrs. Kenworth, is appalled at the idea of Goldie's associating with the lowly Johnny, "this common jockey, this rat of the stable."

Another difficulty is posed by the villainous Englishman Anthony Anstey, who is determined to keep Johnny from winning either the Derby or Goldie. Anstey is in a strong position to cause trouble because he has managed to become engaged to Mrs. Kenworth, which he explains in his cynical worldly fashion: "You must think I'm marrying Mrs. Kenworth because she's got twenty million dollars. Well, I'd marry her if she had forty million."

When Johnny appears in the hotel he struts about and boasts. "I'm a free born American, over twenty-one years of age. I guess I can do anything I please." He announces that victory in the Derby is certain and tells his adoring fans, "Pawn your jewelry, go into hock and play Yankee Doodle straight to win." And then he sings a song about it.

> I'm a Yankee Doodle Dandy
> A Yankee Doodle do or die;
> A real live nephew of my Uncle Sam's,
> Born on the Fourth of July.
>
> I've got a Yankee Doodle sweetheart,
> She's my Yankee Doodle Joy.
> Yankee Doodle came to London,
>     Just to ride the ponies.
> I am a Yankee Doodle Boy!

But Anstey has Johnny's number, for Johnny turns out to be less knowing than he thinks he is. Anstey shows Johnny a letter, purportedly from Goldie, saying that she is jilting him to marry the Earl of Bloomsbury. Johnny is thrown into despair.

The next scene is at the Derby. King Edward and Queen Alexandra arrive offstage. Anstey circulates among the crowd convincing people that he has evidence Johnny is about to throw the race.

> CHORUS:    He'll lose the race and it's a frame
> We know the blighter that's to blame.
> He bears the name of Little Johnny Jones.

And he does lose. The race announcer's voice: "It's all over. British Boy has won the English Derby, and as for Yankee Doodle, well, he can go back to America in defeat." The crowd boos Johnny when he returns to the paddock. There will be an investigation and Johnny is told: "You'll be ruled off the track until all the facts are made quite clear." The act concludes with Johnny in disgrace.

Act 2 takes place on the pier at Southampton. Johnny is running away and, by not staying for the investigation, virtually admitting his guilt. Everyone has turned against him. Having spent his days at race tracks, Johnny understands how fickle people are. "They're cheerin' at ya one day and spittin' at ya the next."

Just when things seem hopeless, Whitney Wilson, a wise-cracking character who has been hanging about for no apparent reason, tells Johnny that he is actually a Pinkerton detective and has been following Anstey, collecting information about his illegal dealings. He now has enough evidence to force Anstey to confess that he was responsible for Johnny's losing the Derby, but in order to do this Johnny must return to London to clear himself. Johnny agrees to do it and as he watches the ship sail away with Goldie on it, sings, with "infinite sadness," the most famous song from the play.

> Give my regards to Broadway,
> Remember me to Herald Square;
> Tell all the gang at Forty-Second Street

That I will soon be there.
Whisper of how I'm yearning
To mingle with the old time throng;
Give my regards to old Broadway
And say that I'll be there, ere long.

Act 3 takes place in San Francisco. Completely exonerated, Johnny returns home a hero. There are complications to be cleared up, but in time he and Goldie are reunited and engaged to be married. Down comes the curtain to a refrain sung by the entire company:

Yankee Doodle went to London
Just to ride the ponies.
I am that Yankee Doodle Boy.
I am that Yankee Doodle Boy.

Cohan called *Little Johnny Jones* a "comedy melodrama." Some of its comedy comes from its farcical treatment of the transatlantic theme, rich heiress, wicked European; but some comes from a popular cultural theme of the time: the bad boy who challenges adults and gets away with it. Cohan understood this aspect of his own character. He proudly described himself as a "fresh guy, a know-it-all, and a smart kid."[3] And he sympathized with this aspect of Tod Sloan's character because there was much of Tod in him. Both might have stepped from the pages of an immensely popular book of the time, *Peck's Bad Boy and His Pa*, by George W. Peck, a book which, with its many sequels, ran through innumerable editions. Cohan *was* the bad boy, Hennery Peck, a brat who spread mayhem and misery all about him, an oedipal riot, a pugnacious defier of authority. Cohan scored his first acting success in the dramatization of *Peck's Bad Boy*. Audiences roared with pleasure as George/Hennery heaped indignities on the adults on stage, and George soaked up their approval. Throughout his career Cohan fought with almost everyone he encountered: his father, other writers, producers, actors, critics.[4]

*Little Johnny Jones* contained some of Cohan's most memorable songs, but it closed after fifty-two performances. However, Cohen didn't give up; he revised it, took it on tour, brought it back to Broadway in May 1905 for a successful run through the fall. And that was the end. Or so it seemed. While historians had not overlooked Cohan's work, the prevailing attitude had been one of disparagement; it was called "vulgar, cheap, ill-mannered, flashily dressed, insolent." (The same things had been said of Diamond Jim Brady and Tod Sloan.) But in the 1980s *Little Johnny Jones* was revived, and it became the subject of scholarly and popular attention; and an authority on American musical theater could praise it as "the piece that most obviously provided the foundation of American musical comedy."[5]

It was no doubt flattering to Tod Sloan to be the subject of a Cohan production, but his own material prospects were not improved by someone else telling his story. So he continued to move from amusement to amusement, from place to place, from failure to failure. Meanwhile, the racing scene he had known was slipping away. In the first decade of the twentieth century, William Whitney, Philip Dwyer, and Lord William Beresford died. Then, in 1910, came the greatest blow: King Edward died. It may have been this event that made Tod recognize that he could once more appear before the racing public, by telling his own story.

He couldn't actually do it entirely "by himself"; he dictated his reminiscences to A. Dick Luckman, a sympathetic English racing journalist. The result was *Tod Sloan by Himself*, first published in England in 1915 and reprinted in America at the end of that year. The publication of the book in the United States prompted a two-page illustrated biographical article in the Sunday *New York Times* magazine. By then the Great War had overtaken Tod, and racing, and England, and all of Europe. Incidents in the career of a jockey couldn't help but seem distant, if not trivial. While Tod was described as the "premiere jockey of the

Sloan served in the French ambulance corps for
a year during World War I. He had volunteered
as a sharpshooter but was turned down because
he was too small.

world," with a name "known to thousands who know nothing
whatever about the turf," the author of the account assumed that
Tod was by then a somewhat shadowy figure; so he zestfully detailed the "Amazing Career of the Indiana Boy Who Rode for
Edward VII." The troubles of 1900 were mentioned—"clouds
began to gather" and Sloan was soon "at loggerheads with En-

glish racing authorities"—and then passed over. The article concluded with a picture of Tod in the uniform of the French ambulance corps, loyally serving the Allies.[6]

*Tod Sloan by Himself* isn't one story but many, a book of events and incidents, anecdotes and biographical snapshots about races and horses, people and places, most of them from Tod's English and European years. Loosely chronological, with few specific dates, the narrative has a curiously timeless flow to it. The early chapters about his boyhood and first riding ventures are especially fresh and compelling. Modest about his achievements, he makes no claim for the importance of the forward seat and is content merely to describe his "invention" of it.

Readers must have been surprised, when the book appeared, that it wasn't, as might have been expected, aimed at personal vindication. There could be no vindication unless, at the very least, allegations were spelled out and detailed evidence brought forward to refute them. But that is not the aim of Tod's memoirs; nor are they a confession of error or a plea for forgiveness. Tod continually almost confesses and then denies that there is anything to confess; seems to admit transgressions and then retracts the admissions; accepts blame—"Looking back, I see plainly that there are plenty of things to blame myself for"[7]—without specifying what it is for.

Among the stories is an account of the Codoman affair. "A whole combination of circumstances" led up to the decision by the Jockey Club, Tod wrote, and his explanation is circumstantial without being illuminating. Tod insisted that "I'm not going to excuse myself for breaking a rule" about betting but then did more or less excuse himself because "many jockeys have sinned with regard to an odd wager or two." His betting was not a thing he could face up to. It led him into an absurd suggestion that if only the Prince of Wales had been able to keep his agreement to have Tod ride for him, "I am sure I shouldn't have given way to the temptation to get about so much and, well, back horses." In fact, he had been, well, backing horses for years before that. And even a moment of self-knowledge comes as an offhand comment about "the gambling habit I could not cure myself of."[8]

*Tod Sloan by Himself* is a clear statement of what he assumes to be a realistic view of the world; his evasiveness about ethical and moral issues is a fundamental part of that statement. It is a book frozen in the values of 1890s racing culture and not of the reformed racing of the time of its writing. It is as detached in its view of human nature and human motivations as Pittsburgh Phil's book about betting. This explains why Tod apparently never resented the almost uncontrolled power of the Jockey Club. His experience of life made it clear that *someone* would be wielding power. The powerless, in all walks of life, simply had to learn to live with the consequences of this state of affairs; and no one understood this better than little men. To survive, jockeys learned "the discretion of silence."[9]

The treatment of the Codoman affair in the memoirs, as being neither more nor less important than many other races, is in keeping with this realistic view. "There was the usual talk about my having done this, that and the other, but I looked upon it quite as an ordinary race." The good thing "hadn't come off; that's all." Of course all jockeys bet. "The allurement is too strong—too strong for human nature." Tod accepted the freckled ambiguity of that nature and therefore of judgments about right and wrong. "Those who go racing know many of the conditions of life." He didn't snivel, and he didn't snitch. Remember that vaudeville joke about Snapper Garrison refusing to say what he did when he was riding: "Tell them what I did? Why I wouldn't do that for ten thousand a week." And he didn't repent, except in one sense: "I have repented I was such a fool."[10] Fools get caught.

There is a moment, however, when the voice of the stoic realist gives way to that of the Hoosier kid deeply pained by the experience of life. At the very end of the memoirs he cries out that "those people," his critics, didn't realize that "after the death of Lord William Beresford and Mr. Whitney I never had as a serious adviser any good powerful friend who [could] put his hand on my shoulder and counsel me what to do."[11] Defiant, on his own, he had also yearned for the authority of that missing father.

In the 1920s another writer found in Tod Sloan's life the subject for a story. Ernest Hemingway's "My Old Man" is about a father and son. Hemingway knew about Tod Sloan, the monkey seat, and the jockey's reputation. Perhaps he had read Tod's memoirs. Writing to his publisher, Charles Scribner, he related an experience he had in riding to a hunt. "I wanted very long stirrups, which astounded [everyone]. The officers of the regiment were measuring my stirrup lengths and comparing them with how Tod Sloane and other notorious American characters used to ride."[12]

While writing the story in Paris soon after World War I, Hemingway frequented places where Tod Sloan was remembered. In 1914, Tod bought a bar in Paris, on the rue Danou, from a former jockey named Milton Henry. "The new proprietor says he has ceased all interest in racing," a newspaper story reported, "and will assume the active management of his establishment."[13] Tod's management didn't last long, but among the bartenders he employed was a Scotsman, Harry MacElhone, who eventually bought the bar and renamed it Harry's Bar. It became popular with American tourists and expatriates in the 1920s, among them Ernest Hemingway, who might well have been regaled by MacElhone with Tod Sloan stories.

"My Old Man" is the story of Joe, a young boy who is living a hand-to-mouth but carefree life, wandering across Italy and France, soon after the war, with his father, a once famous steeplechase jockey known to us only as Butler. In those Paris years Hemingway created a writing style that looked back to the vernacular language and rhythms of Mark Twain and used this beautifully to convey the freshness of a boy's vision of early morning, "with the dew all over everything and the sun just starting to get going"; or of Maisons-Lafitte, near Paris, where Joe roams the countryside, a James Whitcomb Riley idyll in France.

> The town ain't so much, but there's a lake and a swell
> forest that we used to go off bumming in all day, a
> couple of us kids, and my old man made me a sling
> shot and we got a lot of things with it but the best one
> was a magpie. Young Dick Atkinson shot a rabbit
> with it one day and we put it under a tree and were all
> sitting around and Dick had some cigarettes and all of
> a sudden the rabbit jumped up and beat it into the
> brush and we chased it but we couldn't find it. Gee,
> we had fun at Maisons.

But the fun can't last. Humans intrude on nature. Butler had once ridden in the biggest races and is contemptuous of the second-rate racing he is reduced to. There has been some trouble in Butler's past, something unexplained, which brought him low and still hangs ominously about him. Hemingway dramatized the two sides of Tod Sloan, the innocent boy who became the all-too-knowing jockey man, through the figure of the father who shields his son from the threatening reality of the world but also introduces him to it. Butler is the agent of human wickedness, a man inescapably bound to wrongdoing, a prisoner of his own life's experience.

Two racing incidents convey what Joe learns about the world, and how he learns it. At the St. Cloud race course Joe is enchanted by Kzar, the favorite in the big race, "a great big yellow horse that looks like nothing but run. He was so beautiful and he went around the paddock putting his feet just so and quiet and careful and not jerking and standing up on his legs and getting wild eyed like you see these selling platers with a shot of dope in them." But this is a horse race, and we shift from natural beauty to human greed and contrivance. Kzar's rider is George Gardner, Butler's good friend. (Remember: Frank Gardner was

Tod Sloan's friend who gave him the gratuity.) Before the race, in the jockey's dressing room, unknown to Joe, Gardner tells Butler that Kircubbin will win the race, and "kidding like," says to him, "don't bet on anything I tell you." Butler of course puts all his money on Kircubbin.

Hemingway brings the race excitingly to life. The horses come into the home stretch in a bunch, with Kircubbin leading. "Then everybody began to yell Kzar as though they were crazy" and Kzar comes on "faster than I'd ever seen anything in my life, like a yellow streak." Neck and neck, nose and nose at the finish line, Kircubbin wins.

"Wasn't it a swell race, Dad?"

"He looked at me sort of funny with his derby on the back of his head. 'George Gardner's a swell jockey, all right,' he said. 'It sure took a great jock to keep that Kzar horse from winning.'"

Later, Joe reflects on what his old man had said. "That sure took the kick out of it for me and I didn't get the real kick back again ever."

Because of the troubles he had been implicated in earlier, Butler had lost his license to ride. Now he is reinstated. (What if Tod Sloan had been reinstated?) Butler buys a horse named Gilford, to train and to ride, and he immediately begins setting things up for a big payoff. He rides Gilford in a tune-up race, and finishes third. So when the next race is set, one that really matters to Butler, Gilford goes off at long odds.

Butler has staked all he has on Gilford and this time rides as honest and strong a race as he knows how. Hemingway again captures the beauty of the horses' movement, "going nice and sweet and easy" as they come by the grandstand. "I hollered at my old man as he went by and he was leading by about a length and riding way out, and light as a monkey." And then there is a fall, and pileup at one of the barriers, and terrible confusion. Several horses go down, Gilford among them. Butler is thrown, and killed.

George Gardner is in the stands with Joe. They wait together. The stable boys bring back a stretcher with Butler's body on it. (Remember Tod Sloan's words when he fell while riding Ed Stanley in San Francisco: "It happens, it happens. There's nothing to talk about.") Gardner takes Joe away. As they're leaving the track they hear two men bitterly damning Butler. "The crook. He had it coming to him on the stuff he's pulled."

That's the end of the story. Butler had pulled some stuff, and so had Tod Sloan. Gardner tells Joe, "Don't listen to what those bums said. Your old man was one swell guy." Joe's response might well have been Tod Sloan's. "Seems when they get started they don't leave a guy nothing."

Stories. Frank Graham, a New York sportswriter, called his story about Tod "Broke or Not, the Best." Graham remembered the high-living Dandy. The sporting world "had known fast men with a dollar; maybe the fastest of all was Tod Sloan," who, in his palmy days, "had worn the best clothes, smoked the best cigars, drunk the best liquors, eaten the best food." Even when his money disappeared he was still Tod Sloan. "Headwaiters bowed to him in Broadway restaurants and people turned to look at him in the streets and he bought drinks for millionaires and he didn't have a dime."[14]

Jack Doyle's story. A gambler and Broadway character, down on his luck, Doyle lived with Tod for a while. The two of them were reduced to winning bets in pool rooms, but Tod's self-possession was entirely unshaken, as Doyle learned. Once Tod spent their last three dollars on fifty-cent cigars. When Doyle remonstrated, Sloan replied, "John, what good is three dollars?" Another time they won eleven dollars at the track and Tod insisted they celebrate. A cab to a restaurant. (One dollar.) Tod ordered dinner—"No king could order a dinner better than Tod"—then excused himself to step into the kitchen to tell the chef how to prepare some dishes. Fifteen minutes passed. No Sloan. Doyle became uneasy. "Kitchen, my eye. That little sucker probably is in the bar spending our money buying drinks for

Sloan in jodhpurs. "Seems when they get
started they don't leave a guy nothing."

some of his rich friends." Doyle went to the bar. There was Tod, "with a bunch of wealthy guys standing around him and the checks piling up in front of him because he wouldn't let anyone else buy him a drink." (Four dollars.) Six dollars left. Just enough to pay for dinner. "I gave our last quarter to the hat-check girl and there we were on the sidewalk, broke again."[15]

Tod continued to enjoy the company of women. In 1920, after a ten-day courtship, he married again, another actress, Elizabeth Saxon Malone. Hundreds of his friends showed up unexpectedly at his hotel to go to the church with the couple, "a quaint little pair," a newspaperman reported. She weighed 88 pounds and came to just a little above his shoulder; he weighed 125 pounds (no featherweight now). Seven years later Betty Sloan got a divorce, charging Tod with mental cruelty inflicted on her by his "habitual intemperance." She gained custody of their five-year-old daughter.[16]

A life of incessant movement—a racing adage held that "you can't settle down and be a racing man too; it's one or the other"—brought him back to California in the 1920s, which provoked memories by one old turfman of the San Francisco years of the 1890s, those days of growing fame, Tod at the Baldwin Hotel in San Francisco, "the center of all eyes then, just as Jack Dempsey is today." Now he found himself in southern California, hard up, on the ropes, down but not yet out, hoping to hook on to something in Hollywood. The movie colony's racing crowd knew who he was or, at least, who he had been. He got some parts in films and could be seen chatting with Harold Lloyd and Buster Keaton. He attracted some publicity by taking part in goofy stunts: acting as starter for a turtle race, putting on the gloves with Primo Carnera, the heavyweight boxer, two physical freaks, the hulking giant and the aged pygmy, two men forever defined by their size. It was meant to be amusing, but looking at the photograph one feels the poignancy of Tod Sloan ending up where he began, in the carnival world of old Professor Talbot, the balloonist.[17]

Tod Sloan in Hollywood, putting on the
gloves with Primo Carnera. Department of
Special Collections, Charles E. Young
Research Library, University of California,
Los Angeles.

Tod worked at the race track in Tijuana, Mexico, "the
chubby gnome who took your ticket at the paddock gate." That
was where Damon Runyon, sportswriter turned storyteller
about the guys and dolls of the Manhattan underworld, encountered him, resulting in a final bittersweet anecdote. "There
was Tod Sloan," Runyon reported. "A gateman. A bit heavier, but
still able to smile with a nonchalant toss of the head." Tod gave
Runyon a tip on a horse. Runyon didn't take it. The horse lost.[18]

In November 1933 he became gravely ill with cirrhosis of
the liver. A family in Los Angeles was taking care of him. Again
his name was in the newspapers. The *Los Angeles Times* in its story

struck a portentous note. "He rode from obscurity and poverty to acclaim and wealth and then he rode back to poverty and obscurity again. Now he waits for his last mount—the pale steed of death."[19] Tod rallied. "I'm not as near death as they said I was," he insisted, and boasted that he had a couple of gold mines in northern California that would soon prove to be winners. In the meantime, cockily defiant, he ordered a box of long black cigars. He died on December 21, 1933, in the Sylvan Lodge Hospital in Los Angeles.

Sadly, but commonly, while he couldn't repeat his successes, he continually repeated his mistakes. Still he had also done uncommon things, things remembered a century later; and as the title of his memoirs proudly proclaimed in its double meaning, he had done them, a little man taking on the world, by himself. The *New York Times* ticked off some of those memorable things: the Hoosier boy who had a "sensational career," in two countries, who "began a new riding style" and "exerted a peculiar power over his horses" while making and losing a fortune. There were several paragraphs dotted with details of dubious accuracy, Tod Sloan, as ever, entangled in the ambiguities of the past.[20]

A more appropriate obituary had been written some years earlier, when Tod's old friend George Cohan told the story of *his* life, ending with words from *Peck's Bad Boy:* "And so he snuck off, all alone by himself, and nobody didn't see him no more."[21]

# NOTES

The indispensable source for Tod Sloan's life is of course his memoirs, Tod Sloan, *Tod Sloan by Himself* (London, 1915), published by Grant Richards, edited and with an introduction by A. Dick Luckman, and with thirty-three illustrations. The memoirs have been reprinted by San Diego State University Press, Tod Sloan, *Tod Sloan by Himself* (1988), with Luckman's introduction and with all the original illustrations and an anonymous "preface" by John Dizikes. All references in my text are from this edition.

*Epigraphs:* Marcel Proust, *The Guermantes Way,* vol. 1 of *Remembrance of Things Past* (New York, 1934), 761–62. William Makepeace Thackeray, "Steele" in *The English Humorists of the Eighteenth Century* (London, 1901), 387. David Cecil, *Max, A Biography* (London, 1964), 392–93.

ONE Names

1. *Tod Sloan by Himself,* 1.
2. Mark Twain, *The Adventures of Tom Sawyer,* chapter 6.
3. Horace Wade, *Tales of the Turf* (New York, 1956), 145. *Tod Sloan by Himself,* 5.
4. *Tod Sloan by Himself,* 5–6.
5. *Tod Sloan by Himself,* 6–8.

6. *Tod Sloan by Himself,* 8. Robert I. Warshow, *Bet-a-Million Gates: The Story of a Plunger* (New York, 1932), 21–22.

7. Harry Brolaski, *Easy Money, Being the Experiences of a Reformed Gambler* (Cleveland, 1911), 237. Saul Bellow, "A Talk with the Yellow Kid," in *It All Adds Up: From The Dim Past to the Uncertain Future* (New York, 1994), 47–53.

8. *Tod Sloan by Himself,* 6–10.

9. *Tod Sloan by Himself,* 11–14, 48–49. Samuel C. Hildreth and James R. Crowell, *The Spell of the Turf: The Story of American Racing* (Philadelphia, 1926), 120–21.

## two History

1. The trainer was J. Huggins, quoted in George Lambton, *Men and Horses I Have Known* (London, 1924), 253–54.

2. Anita Leslie, *The Remarkable Mr. Jerome* (New York, 1954), 59–60, 76–80. Roger Longrigg, *The History of Horse Racing* (New York, 1972), 223.

3. George Waller, *Saratoga: Saga of an Impious Era* (Englewood Cliffs, N.J., 1966), 127. Stephen Longstreet, *Win or Lose: A Social History of Gambling in America* (Indianapolis, 1977), 62, 66–68.

## three Gambling

1. Henry Chafetz, *Play the Devil: A History of Gambling in the United States from 1492 to 1955* (New York, 1960), 262.

2. *San Francisco Chronicle,* December 10, 1892. Warshow, *Bet-a-Million Gates,* 1–25, 52.

3. Chafetz, *Play the Devil,* 377.

4. Richard Sasuly, *Bookies and Bettors: Two Hundred Years of Gambling* (New York, 1982), 97.

5. Leslie, *Remarkable Mr. Jerome,* 80. Brolaski, *Easy Money,* 9.

## four Jockeys

1. Wray Vamplew, *The Turf: A Social and Economic History of Horse Racing* (London, 1976), 167. *London Sporting Times,* as quoted in *Spirit of the Times,* October 28, 1898.

2. *Spirit of the Times,* May 21, 1898.

3. *San Francisco Chronicle,* April 4, 1896. Dan M. Bowmar III, *Giants of the Turf: The Alexanders, the Belmonts, James R. Keene, the Whitneys* (Lexington, Ky., 1960), 126.

4. *Spirit of the Times,* September 26, 1896.

5. David Alexander, *A Sound of Horses: The World of Racing, from Eclipse to Kelso* (Indianapolis, 1966), 172–74. *Spirit of the Times,* December 15, 1894.

6. *New York Sportsman,* August 27, 1887. *Spirit of the Times,* February 15 and 22, 1896.

7. *New York Sun,* December 3, 1900. *San Francisco Chronicle,* June 19, 1895. *Spirit of the Times,* July 6, 1895.

8. Winnie O'Connor, *Jockeys, Crooks and Kings: The Story of Winnie O'Connor's Life as Told to Earl Chapin May* (New York, 1930), 1–8. Alexander, *Sound of Horses,* 171–72.

9. *Spirit of the Times,* August 4, 1894.

10. O'Connor, *Jockeys, Crooks and Kings,* 7–10.

11. O'Connor, *Jockeys, Crooks and Kings,* 22–23.

12. Edward Cole, ed., *Racing Maxims and Methods of "Pittsburgh Phil" (George E. Smith),* (New York, 1908), 119. *Spirit of the Times,* August 11, 1894.

13. *Spirit of the Times,* June 8, 1895. O'Connor, *Jockeys, Crooks and Kings,* 15. *San Francisco Chronicle,* April 9, 1895. *New York Times,* May 19, 1898.

14. *Spirit of the Times,* June 8, 1895.

15. O'Connor, *Jockeys, Crooks and Kings,* 11–15, 35–36. Chafetz, *Play the Devil,* 378.

16. O'Connor, *Jockeys, Crooks and Kings,* 35–44. William H. P. Robertson, *The History of Thoroughbred Racing in America,* 2 vols. (Englewood Cliffs, N.J., 1964), 1:194.

FIVE  California

1. Robertson, *History of Thoroughbred Racing,* 1:82.

2. C. B. Glasscock, *Lucky Baldwin: The Story of an Unconventional Success* (New York, 1935), 152.

3. *San Francisco Chronicle,* February 27 and March 20, 1895; January 2 and June 1, 1896. *San Francisco Evening Bulletin,* November 24,

1894. *Spirit of the Times,* February 24, 1893, and April 4, 1896. Brolaski, *Easy Money,* 9.

    4. *San Francisco Chronicle,* April 14 and February 23, 1895.

    5. *San Francisco Chronicle,* February 16, 1895; January 17, 1896; January 27, 1895.

    6. *San Francisco Chronicle,* January 2, 5, 10, 11, and 12, 1894.

    7. *San Francisco Chronicle,* January 13, 1894. Vamplew, *Turf,* 168–69.

    8. *San Francisco Chronicle,* February 1 and 13, and March 2, 1894.

    9. *San Francisco Chronicle,* March 20 and 23, 1894.

    10. *San Francisco Chronicle,* April 4, 6, and 21, 1895.

    11. Glenn G. Boyer, ed., *I Married Wyatt Earp: The Recollections of Josephine Sarah Marcus Earp* (Tucson, Ariz., 1976), 144.

    12. *San Francisco Chronicle,* April 4 and May 8, 9, 11, 21, 1895.

## six  Forward Seat

    1. *Tod Sloan by Himself,* 14.

    2. "Notes," *Badminton Magazine,* January 1899, 26–27.

    3. Lambton, *Men and Horses,* 242.

    4. *Tod Sloan by Himself,* 90. *Spirit of the Times,* September 22, 1900.

    5. Lambton, *Men and Horses,* 241–42.

    6. S. Sidney, *The Book of the Horse* (1875), as quoted in Longrigg, *History of Horse Racing,* 224.

    7. Arthur R. Ashe, Jr., *A Hard Road to Glory: A History of the African-American Athlete,* 1619–1918 (New York, 1988), 47–48. *New York Sportsman,* June 28, 1890. Edward Hotaling, "When Racing Colors Included Black," *New York Times,* June 2, 1996.

    8. *New York Sun,* December 3, 1900.

    9. *Spirit of the Times,* January 5, 1901.

    10. *San Francisco Chronicle,* March 29, 1895.

    11. *New York Times,* May 8, 1898.

## seven  Gay Nineties

    1. Robertson, *History of Thoroughbred Racing,* 148–51.

    2. Parker Morell, *Diamond Jim: The Life and Times of James Buchanan Brady* (New York, 1934), 57.

3. Morell, *Diamond Jim*, 213.

4. Morell, *Diamond Jim*, 233. Albert Stevens Crockett, *Peacocks on Parade: A Narrative of a Unique Period in American Social History and Its Most Colorful Figures* (New York, 1931), 300–314.

5. Crockett, *Peacocks on Parade*, 159, 215.

6. Morell, *Diamond Jim*, 23, 36–39, 58–59. Crockett, *Peacocks on Parade*, 211–212.

7. Morell, *Diamond Jim*, 215.

8. *Tod Sloan by Himself*, 3.

9. Robertson, *History of Thoroughbred Racing*, 104, 181, 127–130.

10. Robertson, *History of Thoroughbred Racing*, 146–47, 157–59, 130–37. Morell, *Diamond Jim*, 173, 200, 221–27. *New York Times*, December 1, 1918.

11. *New York Times*, as quoted in Bowmar, *Giants of the Turf*, 126.

12. Robertson, *History of Thoroughbred Racing*, 195.

13. Robertson, *History of Thoroughbred Racing*, 175.

### EIGHT Mastery

1. *New York Herald*, July 25, May 18, and June 17, 1896.

2. *New York Herald*, July 12, 1896. *New York Herald*, June 26, 1898. *New York Herald*, June 19, 1896. *New York Times*, July 3, 1896.

3. *New York Times*, July 3, 1896.

4. *New York Herald*, June 6, 13, and 17, and July 8, 1897.

5. *New York Sun*, July 6, 1897. *New York Sun*, August 19, 1897. *New York Herald*, June 9, 1898. *New York Sun*, July 9 and September 26, 1898. *New York Sun*, September 5, 1897.

6. *New York Sun*, June 3, July 8, September 3, and May 23, 1898.

7. *New York Herald*, June 5, 1896. *New York Herald*, June 17 and 19, 1897. *New York Sun*, August 8 and September 15, 1897.

8. *New York Herald*, June 7 and 22, 1897.

9. *New York Times*, May 8, 1898.

10. *New York Herald*, July 3 and 4, 1896.

11. Cole, *Racing Maxims of "Pittsburgh Phil,"* 13.

12. Cole, *Racing Maxims of "Pittsburgh Phil,"* 31, 123.

13. Cole, *Racing Maxims of "Pittsburgh Phil,"* 84–91.

14. Cole, *Racing Maxims of "Pittsburgh Phil,"* 88–90.

15. James C. McGill as told to Clem McCarthy, "Pittsburgh Phil,

'Who Made a Killing at the Races until the Races Killed Him,' " *Saturday Evening Post,* August 3, 1940, 9–11, 74–76; August 10, 1940, 24–25, 68–71; August 17, 1940, 24–25, 51, 53–54.

    16.  *Tod Sloan by Himself,* 20.

    17.  McGill, "Pittsburgh Phil," *Saturday Evening Post,* August 10, 1940, 71.

    18.  *New York Times,* June 8, 9, 11, 15, 16, and 17, 1898. *New York Times,* May 21, 1898. *Spirit of the Times,* May 21, 1898.

    19.  *Spirit of the Times,* June 11, 1898. *Tod Sloan by Himself,* 54.

## NINE  England

    1.  *Tod Sloan by Himself,* 29. Bowmar, *Giants of the Turf,* 117.

    2.  Vamplew, *The Turf,* 142, 133.

    3.  Virginia Cowles, *Gay Monarch* (New York, 1956), 189–221. Philippe Jullian, *Edward and the Edwardians* (New York, 1967), 116–24.

    4.  Jullian, *Edward and the Edwardians,* 147. Cowles, *Gay Monarch,* 209–11. Roger Mortimer, *The Jockey Club* (London, 1958), 118–22.

    5.  Ernest Bland, ed., "The Jockey Club," in *Flat-Racing Since 1900* (London, 1950), 15–32. Vamplew, *The Turf,* 80. Mortimer, *Jockey Club,* 35–46.

    6.  Vamplew, *The Turf,* 77.

    7.  Lambton, *Men and Horses,* 250–51.

    8.  "The American Jockey Invasion," *Badminton Magazine,* April 1907, 422–33.

## TEN  Monkey Seat

    1.  *Tod Sloan by Himself,* 29–30.

    2.  *Sporting Life,* October 11, 1897.

    3.  "The American Jockey Invasion," *Badminton Magazine,* April 1907, 422–33.

    4.  "American Jockey Invasion," 425.

    5.  "D. Maher on Race-Riding," *Badminton Magazine,* May 1905, 556. *The Times,* October 28, 1897. *Sportsman,* October 30, 1897. *Sporting Life,* October 30, 1897.

    6.  "Notes," *Badminton Magazine,* February 1901, 232–34. "American Jockey Invasion," 425–26. *Sporting Life,* October 30, 1897.

7. *Tod Sloan by Himself,* 42–43. *The Referee,* as quoted in *Spirit of the Times,* November 27, 1897. *The Times,*November 20, 1897. *New York Times,* January 23, 1898.

8. *Sporting Life,* October 1, 1898.

9. *Sporting Life,* September 23 and October 1, 1898.

10. "American Jockey Invasion," 426–28. *Tod Sloan by Himself,* 63–65.

11. *Sporting Life,* October 4, 1898.

12. *Daily Mail, Daily Telegraph, Sporting Life,* as quoted in *Spirit of the Times,* November 6 and 13, 1897.

13. *Tod Sloan by Himself,* 65–66, 88–90.

14. Lambton, *Men and Horses,* 190. *Tod Sloan by Himself,* 83–86. *New York Times,* June 1, 1899. *New York Times,* June 1 and 4, 1899.

15. "Notes," *Badminton Magazine,* January 1899, 26.

16. *Tod Sloan by Himself,* 55.

17. *Tod Sloan by Himself,* 56–61.

18. *Tod Sloan by Himself,* 1, 55–56, 61.

19. *Sporting Life,* October 1, 1898.

20. *Spirit of the Times,* December 24, 1898.

21. *Tod Sloan by Himself,* 54.

22. *Spirit of the Times,* November 6, 1897.

ELEVEN  Yankee Doodle

1. Lambton, *Men and Horses,* 242, 244–45. *Tod Sloan by Himself,* 66.

2. *Tod Sloan by Himself,* 65–66.

3. *Tod Sloan by Himself,* 67–68.

4. *Tod Sloan by Himself,* 95. Alexander, *Sound of Horses,* 174. Lambton, *Men and Horses,* 214.

5. Lambton, *Men and Horses,* 242–44.

6. *Tod Sloan by Himself,* 78–80. Lambton, *Men and Horses,* 247.

7. Lambton, *Men and Horses,* 247–48.

8. *New York Sun,* May 29, 1898. *New York Times,* May 29, 1898.

9. *New York Times,* July 2, 1898.

10. *New York Times,* May 8, 1898.

11. *Kansas City Star,* October 1, 5, 10, 12, 13, 14, 15, 17, and 18, 1898.

12. Dixon Wechter, *The Saga of American Society: A Record of Social Aspiration, 1607–1937* (1970), 404–16.

13. Alexander, *Sound of Horses*, 173.

14. Longstreet, *Win or Lose*, 66–67. Waller, *Saratoga*, 274. Alexander, *Sound of Horses*, 172. *Tod Sloan by Himself*, 127, 52.

15. Alexander, *Sound of Horses*, 172.

16. *New York Times*, June 17, 18, 20, and 21, 1899. *The Times*, June 17 and 18, 1899. *Tod Sloan by Himself*, 106–9.

17. Barry Campbell, *Horse Racing in Britain* (London, 1977), 123. Vamplew, *The Turf*, 147–51.

18. *Spirit of the Times*, June 5, 1897, 638. Alexander Pope, "The Club of Little Men," as quoted in W. H. Auden, *Forewords and Afterwords* (1974), 116. Vamplew, *The Turf*, 160.

19. Vamplew, *The Turf*, 148. *New York Herald*, August 26, 1900. *New York Sun*, August 26, 1900.

TWELVE **Trouble**

1. *Tod Sloan by Himself*, 92–94. "D. Maher on Race-Riding," *Badminton Magazine*, May 1905, 556.

2. "Notes," *Badminton Magazine*, December 1904, 664. *Spirit of the Times*, December 16, 1899. "American Jockey Invasion," 433.

3. Alfred E. T. Watson, "American Training Methods," *Badminton Magazine*, July 1901, 35–41.

4. Watson, "Training Methods," 37. Lambton, *Men and Horses*, 252–56.

5. Lambton, *Men and Horses*, 260. *Tod Sloan by Himself*, 100.

6. *Spirit of the Times*, February 18 and November 5, 1898.

7. *New York Times*, August 16, 1899.

8. *Spirit of the Times*, September 22, 1900.

9. "American Jockey Invasion," 431–32. *Tod Sloan by Himself*, 114–15.

10. *Tod Sloan by Himself*, 118, 113.

11. *Spirit of the Times*, October 13, 1900.

12. *New York Sun*, August 26, 1900. *New York Herald*, August 26, 1900. *New York Times*, August 26, 1900. *Spirit of the Times*, August 25 and September 1 and 8, 1900. O'Connor, *Jockeys, Crooks and Kings*, 65–66.

13. *Tod Sloan by Himself,* 57. Richard Marsh, *A Trainer to Two Kings* (London, 1925), 155. *Spirit of the Times,* October 13, 1900.

14. *Spirit of the Times,* October 27, 1900.

15. *Spirit of the Times,* October 27, 1900.

16. *Spirit of the Times,* October 27 and November 3, 1900.

17. *Tod Sloan by Himself,* 120.


THIRTEEN Judgment

1. *The Times,* December 6, 1900.

2. *New York Times,* December 7, 1900. *New York Sun,* December 3, 5, 7, and 8, 1900.

3. Letter to the author from the Jockey Club, June 22, 1992.

4. *Spirit of the Times,* December 7, 1900.

5. *New York Herald,* August 26, 1900.

6. *Spirit of the Times,* December 15, 1900.

7. As quoted in *Spirit of the Times,* December 15, 1900. *New York Times,* December 7, 1900.

8. C. R. Acton, *Silk and Spur* (London, 1936), 105–6. Mortimer, *Jockey Club,* 145.

9. *Tod Sloan by Himself,* 103.

10. *Tod Sloan by Himself,* 120.

11. *Tod Sloan by Himself,* 124.

12. *Tod Sloan by Himself,* 125.

13. Wade, *Tales of the Turf,* 148.

14. *Tod Sloan by Himself,* 122–23.

15. *Tod Sloan by Himself,* 129–34.

16. *Tod Sloan by Himself,* 127.

17. Crockett, *Peacocks on Parade,* 269–70.

18. *Tod Sloan by Himself,* 136–39. *New York Times,* May 21, June 9, November 24, and December 15 and 16, 1903.

19. *Tod Sloan by Himself,* 124.


FOURTEEN The Wizard

1. *Tod Sloan by Himself,* 146–47.

2. *Tod Sloan by Himself,* 149. *New York Times,* December 12, 1905.

3. *Tod Sloan by Himself,* 145. *New York Times,* March 15, 1905.

4. *Tod Sloan by Himself,* 146.

5. *Tod Sloan by Himself,* 146. *New York Times,* January 5, February 8, and April 8, 1906.

6. *Tod Sloan by Himself,* 175–76.

7. *Tod Sloan by Himself,* 176.

8. Alva Johnson, *The Legendary Mizners* (New York, 1953), 203–4.

9. *New York Times,* February 28, 1909.

10. *New York Times,* March 6, 1914. *Tod Sloan by Himself,* 147.

11. Public Records Office (London), Home Office, 46, #184, November 6, 1915, CID, Sloan, Tod & D'Herlys, Mad, Repts as dangerous, #368, November 29, 1915. Asst. Commissioner, Sloan, James T. or Tod & Dandirac, Simone, #383, "Reports deportation." *New York Times,* November 24 and 25, 1915.

12. *Tod Sloan by Himself,* 179. *New York Times,* November 24 and 25, 1915.

13. *Tod Sloan by Himself,* 162.

14. Marsh, *Trainer to Two Kings,* 320–22. Harding Cox, *Chasing and Racing* (London, 1922), 211–13.

15. Sidney Galtrey, *Memoirs of a Racing Journalist* (London, 1934), 189–90. Acton, *Silk and Spur,* 112. Joe Palmer, *This Was Racing* (New York, 1953), 236.

16. Lambton, *Men and Horses,* 259–60.

17. Cox, *Chasing and Racing,* 213–14.

18. Vamplew, *The Turf,* 105–7.

19. "Review," *Observer* (London), March 1, 1998.

FIFTEEN  Stories

1. Herman Hesse, *The Glass Bead Game* (New York, 1969), 48.

2. Ward Morehouse, *George M. Cohan: Prince of the American Theater* (New York, 1943), 64.

3. John McCabe, *George M. Cohan: The Man Who Owned Broadway* (New York, 1973), 33.

4. McCabe, *Cohan,* 17–18.

5. McCabe, *Cohan,* xii. Andrew Lamb, *150 Years of Popular Musical Theatre* (New Haven, 2000).

6. *New York Times,* November 28, 1915.

7. *Tod Sloan by Himself,* 113.

8. *Tod Sloan by Himself,* 125, 61, 127.

9. *Tod Sloan by Himself,* 200.

10. *Tod Sloan by Himself,* 118, 61, 147, 203.

11. *Tod Sloan by Himself,* 201.

12. Carlos Baker, ed., *Selected Letters of Ernest Hemingway, 1917–1961* (New York, 1981), 664.

13. *New York Times,* March 6, 1914.

14. Charles B. Parmer, *For Gold and Glory: The Story of Thoroughbred Racing in America* (New York, 1939), 154–58.

15. Parmer, *For Gold and Glory,* 154–58.

16. *New York Times,* June 25, 1920, and November 27, 1927.

17. Hildreth and Crowell, *Spell of the Turf,* 10, 122. Robertson, *History of Thoroughbred Racing,* 1:171.

18. Parmer, *For Gold and Glory,* 15.

19. *Los Angeles Times,* November 29, and December 1, 22, and 27, 1933.

20. *New York Times,* November 29, and December 1, 22, and 27, 1933.

21. George M. Cohan, *Twenty Years on Broadway and the Years It Took to Get There* (New York, 1924), 264.

# BIBLIOGRAPHY

Acton, C. R. *Silk and Spur.* London, 1936.

Alexander, David. *A Sound of Horses: The World of Racing, from Eclipse to Kelso.* Indianapolis, 1966.

Ashe, Arthur R., Jr. *A Hard Road to Glory: A History of the African-American Athlete, 1619–1918.* New York, 1988.

Baker, Carlos, ed. *Selected Letters of Ernest Hemingway, 1917–1961.* New York, 1981.

Bellow, Saul. "A Talk with the Yellow Kid." In *It All Adds Up, From the Dim Past to the Uncertain Future.* New York, 1994.

Bird, T. H. *Admiral Rous and the English Turf.* London, 1939.

Bland, Ernest, ed. *Flat-Racing Since 1900.* London, 1950.

Bowmar, Dan M. III. *Giants of the Turf: The Alexanders, the Belmonts, James R. Keene, the Whitneys.* Lexington, Ky., 1960.

Boyer, Glenn G., ed. *I Married Wyatt Earp: The Recollections of Josephine Sarah Marcus Earp.* Tucson, Ariz., 1976.

Brolaski, Harry. *Easy Money, Being the Experiences of a Reformed Gambler.* Cleveland, 1911.

Burnham, John C. *Bad Habits: Drinking, Smoking, Taking Drugs, Gambling, Sexual Misbehavior, and Swearing in American History.* New York, 1993.

Campbell, Barry. *Horse Racing in Britain.* London, 1977.

Chafetz, Henry. *Play the Devil: A History of Gambling in the United States from 1492 to 1955.* New York, 1960.

Chalmers, P. R. *Racing England.* London, 1939.

Chesney, K. *The Victorian Underworld.* London, 1970.

Cohan, George M. *Twenty Years on Broadway and the Years It Took to Get There.* New York, 1924.

Cohen, John. *Chance, Skill, and Luck: The Psychology of Guessing and Gambling.* Baltimore, 1960.

Cole, Edward, ed. *Racing Maxims and Methods of "Pittsburgh Phil" (George E. Smith).* New York, 1908.

Cook, T. A. *A History of the English Turf.* 3 vols. London, 1905.

Cowles, Virginia. *Gay Monarch.* New York, 1956.

Cox, Harding. *Chasing and Racing.* London, 1922.

Crockett, Albert Stevens. *Peacocks on Parade: A Narrative of a Unique Period in American Social History and Its Most Colorful Figures.* New York, 1931.

Fabian, Ann. *Card Sharps, Dream Books, and Gambling in Nineteenth-Century America.* Ithaca, 1990.

Fane, M. *Racecourse Swindles.* London, 1936.

Galtrey, Sidney. *Memoirs of a Racing Journalist.* London, 1934.

Glasscock, C. B. *Lucky Baldwin: The Story of an Unconventional Success.* New York, 1935.

Hervey, John. *Racing in America, 1922–1936.* New York, 1937.

Hildreth, Samuel C., and James R. Crowell. *The Spell of the Turf: The Story of American Racing.* Philadelphia, 1926.

Hotaling, Edward. "When Racing Colors Included Black," *New York Times,* June 2, 1996.

Jarvis, Jack. *They're Off.* London, 1969.

Johnson, Alva. *The Legendary Mizners.* New York, 1953.

Jullian, Philippe. *Edward and the Edwardians.* New York, 1967.

Lamb, Andrew. *150 Years of Popular Musical Theatre.* New Haven, 2000.

Lambton, George. *Men and Horses I Have Known.* London, 1924.

Leslie, Anita. *The Remarkable Mr. Jerome.* New York, 1954.

Longrigg, Roger. *The History of Horse Racing.* New York, 1972.

Longstreet, Stephen. *Win or Lose: A Social History of Gambling in America.* Indianapolis, 1977.

McCabe, John. *George M. Cohan: The Man Who Owned Broadway.* New York, 1973.

Marsh, Richard. *A Trainer to Two Kings.* London, 1925.

Morehouse, Ward. *George M. Cohan: Prince of the American Theater.* New York, 1943.

Morell, Parker. *Diamond Jim: The Life and Times of James Buchanan Brady.* New York, 1934.

Mortimer, Roger. *The Jockey Club.* London, 1958.

O'Connor, Winnie. *Jockeys, Crooks and Kings: The Story of Winnie O'Connor's Life as Told to Earl Chapin May.* New York, 1930.

Palmer, Joe. *This Was Racing.* New York, 1953.

Parmer, Charles B. *For Gold and Glory: The Story of Thoroughbred Racing in America.* New York, 1939.

Richardson, Charles. *The English Turf, A Record of Horses and Courses,* ed. by E. T. Sachs. New York, 1901.

Robertson, William H. P. *The History of Thoroughbred Racing in America.* 2 vols. Englewood Cliffs, N.J., 1964.

Sasuly, Richard. *Bookies and Bettors: Two Hundred Years of Gambling.* New York, 1982.

Sievier, Robert S. *The Autobiography of Robert Standish Sievier.* London, 1906.

Sloan, Tod. *Tod Sloan by Himself.* San Diego, 1988.

Vamplew, Wray. *The Turf: A Social and Economic History of Horse Racing.* London, 1976.

"Vigilant." [Vosburgh, F. W., comp.] *Famous American Jockeys* (n.d.).

Vosburgh, Walter S. *Racing in America, 1866–1921.* New York, 1922.

Wade, Horace. *Tales of the Turf.* New York, 1956.

Waller, George. *Saratoga: Saga of an Impious Era.* Englewood Cliffs, N.J., 1966.

Warshow, Robert I. *Bet-a-Million Gates: The Story of a Plunger.* New York, 1932.

Welcome, J. *Fred Archer: His Life and Times.* London, 1967.

# INDEX

African Americans: and American Derby, 65; and Belmont Stakes, 65; and forward-seat riding, 62–67; as jockeys, 37–38, 62–65; and Kentucky Derby, 65; and Preakness, 65; and prize fighting, 99; and racism, 37–38, 73–74; riding styles of, 62–67; as trainers, 37; winning against Sloan, 67–68

Aldrich, Thomas Bailey, 3

Alexander Park race track, 43

American Derby, 20, 65, 69

American Jockey Club, 17

"American seat." *See* Forward-seat riding

American Turf Association, 168–69

America's Cup, 99

Archer, Fred, 134

Ascot, 132–33, 138

Astor, William Waldorf, 76

Auction pools, 22–23, 24

Australia, 69

Bald, Eddie, 141

Baldwin, Elias Jackson "Lucky," 48–50, 90

Ballooning, 6–9

Bassett, Harry, 60

Bay District race track, 20, 42, 48, 50–52, 69–70, 91

Bay View race track, 48

Belmont, August, 15–16, 17, 29, 78, 82, 131, 181

Belmont Park, 179

Belmont Stakes, 65, 66, 72

Beresford, Lord Marcus, 117, 149

Beresford, Lord William, 109, 114, 117, 133, 153, 189, 193

Betting. *See* Gambling

Billiards, 23, 169

Blauser family, 1–5

217

Board of Control, 81

Bookmakers: and agents, 90; and corruption at race track, 26–27; in England, 21, 141; and fixed races, 51–52; and inside information, 26; and pari-mutuel system, 22, 180; power of, 27–28; and race track attendance, 53; Sloan as, 170; wagering system of, 23–24; women as, 23. *See also* Gambling

"Bottom," 14

Bowie, Ogden, 19–20

Bowling, Tom, 18

Bradley, Edward R., 28

Brady, James Buchanan "Diamond Jim," 74–78, 80

Brighton Beach race track, 38, 72, 84

"Broke or Not, the Best" (Graham), 196

Brooklyn Handicap, 72, 76, 127

Brooklyn Jockey Club, 28, 156

California Jockey Club, 51

Cambridgeshire, 105, 108–9, 143

Campbell, Jimmy, 10

Canfield, Richard, 75, 148–49

Capitalism, 13–16

Carr, Felix, 42

Cella, Louis, 27

Central Park race track, 29

Cesarwitch, 104, 105

Champagne Stakes, 72

Cheating, 181

Chester Cup, 181

Chetwynd, George, 176

Chevalier, 37

Chifney, Sam, 102–3

Churchill, Lord Randolph, 129

Churchill Downs Race Course, 20

Civil War, 15, 98

Clifton, Lord Talbot, 48

Cocaine, 45, 137

Codoman affair, 142–44, 156–57, 191–92

Cohan, George M., 167, 183–85, 200

Cole, Edward W., 90, 91

Coney Island Jockey Club, 72, 95

Corrigan, Ed, 34, 81, 139, 168–69

Coughlin, Bath House John, 28

Coventry, Arthur, 115

Covington, Aleck, 40

Cox, Harding, 174

Cribb, Tom, 99

Crocker, William, 48

Croker, Richard, 28, 144

Daly, Bill "Father," 38–39, 41–42

Daly, Marcus, 79, 89

Daly, Mike, 38

Dana, Richard Henry, 47

Defense of the Realm Act of Great Britain, 173

Derby, 100, 102, 104, 105, 114–16, 136

Digitalis, 45

Doping horses, 34, 42, 43, 45, 52–53, 137–39, 181

Doyle, Jack, 196, 198

Drunkenness, 36–37, 40

Dunn, Finley Peter, 129

Durham, Lord, 144, 149–51, 160, 176
Dwyer, Charles, 139
Dwyer, Mike, 27–28, 72–73, 79–80, 90, 180
Dwyer, Philip J., 27–28, 72–73, 75, 79–80, 156, 158, 180, 189

Earp, Wyatt, 56
Eclipse Stakes, 95
Edward, Prince of Wales and King of England, 101–3, 116–18, 131, 149, 151, 156, 160–61, 172, 189, 191
Electric Light Park, 46
Electrical shocks, 44–45
England: Act for the Suppression of Betting Houses, 21; and American gamblers, 139–40; anti-Americanism in, 137–39, 144–45, 149–50, 160; bookmakers in, 21, 141; and forward-seat riding, 66, 112–14; horse racing in, 14, 97–134; racing seasons in, 14; riding styles in, 66; starting gates in, 69. See also Jockey Club
Epsom Gold Cup, 105

Fair Grounds, 20
Fallon, Kieren, 181–82
Farewell Handicap, 110
Fitzsimmons, Bob, 75
Flynn, Willie, 41, 42
Football, 98
Forward-seat riding: acceptance of, 84–85, 95; and African

Americans, 62–67; criticism of, 60–61, 83, 115, 136–37; description of, 59; development of, 58–59, 62–65; in England, 66, 112–14; public notice of, 61–62; as revolutionary, 59–60; and Sloan, 58–68, 83, 88–89, 93, 107–8, 174, 191; and winning races, 68
France, 21–22, 37, 142, 165–66
Frazee, Harry, 184
Free Handicap, 109
"French pools," 25
Futurity, 72, 145–48, 156

Galtrey, Sidney, 174
Gambling: agents for, 90; American gamblers in England, 139–40; and attendance at horse races, 178, 180–81; and auction pools, 22–23, 24, 26; and betting rings, 23–24; and bookmakers, 21–24, 26–28, 51–53, 90, 141, 170, 180; and cheating control, 181; and handicapping, 31–33, 34; high-stakes betting, 24–25; and inside information, 26; Jerome on, 30; and jockeys, 32; off-track betting, 180; pari-mutuel system of, 21–22, 25–26, 28, 180; and "pool" halls, 23, 26, 196; prohibition of, 178; scale of wagering in 1894, 72; on Sloan, 85, 86–87; by Sloan, 26, 89–94, 119–20, 123, 140, 142–44, 148–49, 163–65,

Gambling (*cont.*)
  170, 172–73, 175, 191–92,
  196; Smith on, 90; and trainers,
  34–35
Gardner, Frank, 143, 144, 156–
  57, 194–95
Garfield race track, 81
Garrison, Snapper, 168
Gates, John Wayne "Bet-a-Mil-
  lion," 24–25, 53, 75, 90, 139–
  40, 159
Goodwood Cup, 104, 138
Goodwood Stakes, 104
Graham, Frank, 196
Grannan, Riley, 53, 139
Grant, U. S., 17–18
Gravesend race track, 28, 72–73,
  76, 81
Great Depression, 181
Great Lancashire Handicap, 110
Great Metropolitan, 105
Great Tom Stakes, 110
Griffin, Henry, 124

Hall, Joe, 75
Hammerstein, Oscar, 167
Handicapping, 31–33, 34
Hannan, Charlie, 163
Harewood, Lord, 161–62
Harris, Sam, 184
Hawkins, Abe, 65
Hawthorne race track, 81
Hearst, George, 48
Heenan, John C., 99
Held, Anna, 74
Hemingway, Ernest, 193, 196
Henry, Milton, 193
Heroin, 45, 137

Hesse, Herman, 183
Hildreth, Samuel, 11, 79
Homer, Winslow, 2–3
Horse racing: American Derby,
  20; Board of Control, 81; and
  capitalism, 13–16; characteristics of American horse racing,
  14–15; and Civil War, 15; and
  doping horses, 34, 42, 43, 45,
  52–53, 137–39, 181; and electrical shocks to horses, 44–45;
  in England, 14, 97–134; English influence on American
  horse racing, 13, 98–100; expansion of, 71; fixed races, 43–
  46, 51–52, 143–44; and forward-seat riding, 58–70; history of, 12–20, 47–48; injured
  horses, 45, 54; Kentucky
  Derby, 28; and photo finish
  camera, 180; and "plow horses,"
  26; and Progressivism, 177–78;
  and Prohibition, 177–78; quarter-horse racing, 13; and respectability, 28–30; and Revolutionary War, 12–13; and
  "ringer" horses, 43; schedules
  for, 16; seasons for, 14; and
  speed, 179; and stable boys, 9–
  10; technological improvements in, 179–80; and theatrical people, 73–78; and trainers,
  33–35; and transportation of
  horses, 15; and Wall Street people, 74, 78–82; and women,
  16, 18–19, 51; and working
  class, 16. *See also* Gambling;
  Jockeys; Race tracks; Starting;

*and specific jockeys, races, and race tracks*
Howard, E. Phocian, 90
Huggins, J., 63–65, 202n1

Idle Hour farm, 28

Jerome, Leonard, 16, 17, 28–30, 72, 129, 180, 181
Jerome Park race track, 17, 18, 19, 30, 65, 71
Jerome Stakes, 18
Jockey Club: discipline of Sloan, 153–56, 160–62, 166; and doping horses, 139; English version as model for American jockey clubs, 14; founding of, 102; investigations of, 144, 151; power of, 104, 192; rules and procedures of, 43, 103, 138, 176–77. *See also specific jockey clubs*
Jockey Club Stakes, 102
Jockey Guild, 181
Jockeys: African Americans as, 37–38, 62–65; arrests of, 81; character of, 35; and drunkenness, 36–37, 40; emergence of professional jockeys, 31; featherweight jockeys, 31; and fixing races, 43–46; and gambling, 32, 192; honesty of, 40–43, 51; and segregation, 37; size of, 35–36; and snitching, 42; violence of, 35, 39–40, 132–33; weighing of, 36; word origin, 35. *See also* Forward-seat riding; *and specific jockeys*

Jubilee Stakes, 127

Keene, Foxhall, 97–98
Keene, George, 89
Keene, James R., 34, 75, 79, 81–82, 97–98, 105, 106, 108, 145, 147, 148
Kentucky Derby, 24, 65, 66
Kipling, Rudyard, 101

Lambton, George, 115, 125–26, 138, 139
Laudanum, 137
Leonard, Nellie. *See* Russell, Lillian
Leopold, King of Belgium, 131–32
Lewis, Oliver, 65
Lewisohn, Jesse, 80
Lincoln Handicap, 114
*Little Johnny Jones,* 184–89
Liverpool race track, 144
Loates, Tom, 124
Longchamps, 112
Lorillard, Pierre, 16, 26–27, 29, 82, 104–5, 106, 109
Luckman, A. Dick, 189

McCarthy, Clem, 92
McCauley, Edna, 80
McCoy, Kid, 75
McDonald, Michael, 28
MacElhone, Harry, 193
McGill, James C., 92–94
McGraw, John J., 169
McKenna, Hinky Dink, 28
Maher, Danny, 136
Malone, Elizabeth Saxon, 198

Marlborough, Richard John, Duke of, 129–30
Marsh, Richard, 109–10, 174–75
Maspeth race track, 46
Metropolitan Handicap, 72
Metropolitan Turf Associates, 28
Middle Park Plate, 112
Mills, C. A., 154, 157
Mizner, Wilson, 170, 172
Molineaux, Tom, 99
"Monkey seat." See Forward-seat riding
Monmouth Park race track, 27, 71–72, 81
Monte Carlo, 163–65
Morgan, J. P., 25
Morris Park race track, 72, 81, 86–87, 93
Morrissey, John "Old Smoke," 18, 19, 27, 29, 44
Motorcars, 162–63
Murphy, Isaac, 36–37, 41, 65–66
"My Old Man" (Hemingway), 193, 196

National Stallion Stakes, 95
Native Americans, 62
Neil, Frankie, 40
New York Jockey Club, 82
New York Stock Exchange, 28
Newmarket Handicap, 105
Newmarket race track: and Codoman affair, 143, 153; and Edward, Prince of Wales, 116–17; and fixed races, 181; and gambling, 149; and Gardner, 144; importance of, 102; Sloan on, 173; Sloan racing at, 106, 111, 114, 116–17, 134, 143, 144

Oaks, 114
O'Connor, Winnie, 38–40, 42–43, 46, 132, 148
Offenbach, Jacques, 17
Old Cambridgeshire, 110, 116–17
Old Nursery Stakes, 108
Old World riding style, 60
Ollet, Pierre, 25

Pacific Coast Jockey Club, 48
Palmer, Joe, 175
Pari-mutuel betting, 21–22, 25–26, 28, 180
Paris-Mutuels, 25
Peck, George W., 3
Peck's Bad Boy and His Pa (Peck), 3
Penny, Hugh, 40
Photo finish camera, 180
Pimlico race track, 20
Pincus, Jake, 106–7
Pioneer Course, 47
Plessy v. Ferguson, 37
"Plow horses," 26
Poniotowski, Andre, 48
Pool halls, 23, 26, 196
Pope, Alexander, 134
Post delays. See Starting
Preakness, 20, 65, 66
Prince of Wales. See Edward, Prince of Wales
Prix de Diane, 165–66

Prize fighting, 98–99, 134
Progressivism, 177–78
Prohibition, 177–78

Quarter-horse racing, 13
Queens County Jockey Club, 72–73
Queensbury, Marquess of, 99

Race tracks: and betting rings, 23; corruption at, 26–27; life expectancy of, 16–17; and pari-mutuel betting, 21–22, 25–26, 28, 180; and women, 16, 18. *See also specific race tracks*
*Racing Calendar*, 103, 153, 157
*Racing Maxims and Methods of "Pittsburgh Phil"* (Cole), 91
Racism, 37–38, 73–74
Revolutionary War, 12–13, 99
Rickaby, Fred, 124
Reiff, Johnny, 136, 138
Reiff, Lester, 124, 136, 138, 153
Riley, Jamees Whitcomb, 3
"Ringer" horses, 43
Romanov, Duke Michael, 131
Rose, George, 51–52
Rothschild Plate, 110
Rowe, James, 33, 34, 168
Runyon, Damon, 199
Russell, Lillian, 75–76, 80
Ryan, Paddy, 75
Ryan, T. H., 33

Sailing, 98–99
St. Aspach race track, 43
St. Leger, 102, 105, 111

St. Louis race track, 69
San Francisco Jockey Club, 53
Sanderson, Julia, 169
Sanford, Milton, 104
Santa Anita race track, 50
Saratoga race track, 18, 27, 29, 148
Schreiber, Barney, 27
Scribner, Charles, 193
Segregation, 37–38, 73–74
Sheepshead Bay race track, 72, 81, 145–48
Sheridan, Philip, 20
Sherman Anti-Trust Act of *1890*, 82
Simms, Willie, 65–66, 68, 113–14
Slavery, 65. *See also* African Americans
Sloan, Cassius "Cash," 9, 41, 124
Sloan, Elizabeth Saxon Malone, 198
Sloan, James Forman "Tod": and Baldwin, 50; as balloonist, 6–9; as bar owner, 193; as billiard parlor operator, 169; birth of, 1; and Blauser family, 1–5; as bookmaker, 170, 180; British legal charges against Sloan for, 172–73, 175–76; character of, 94, 117, 123–25, 134, 157; childhood of, 1–5; death of, 200; divorces of, 172; education, 4; fashion style of, 88–89, 131, 146; and fear of horses, 10; genius of, 173–75; on Grannan, 139; as horse owner,

Sloan, James Forman "Tod" (*cont.*) 165–66; illness of, 199–200; lawsuits against, 170; marriages of, 169, 172, 198; and Mizner, 170, 172; in Monte Carlo, 163–65; and mother's death, 2; and motorcars, 162–63; as movie stunt man, 198; odd jobs of, 5; other names of, 1; photographs of, 113, 125, 130, 146, 171, 190, 197, 199; physical description of, 5–6; popularity of, 111–12, 128–29; questionable races of, 89–90; racism of, 37–38; and Runyon, 199; and Schreiber, 27; as stable boy, 9–10; stage drama about life of, 184–89; and trap shooting, 163–65; vaudeville act of, 167–68; violence of, 39, 132–33; and women, 88, 128–29, 158, 164, 165, 198; writings of, 2

—gambling: culture of, 26; as jockey, 89–94, 119–20, 123, 140, 142–44, 148–49, 191–92; Jockey Club inquiry and punishment, 144, 156–57; personal gambling after end of jockey career, 163–65, 170, 172–73, 175, 196

—as jockey: and American Turf Association, 168–69; and anti-Americanism in England, 152; Ascot Incident, 132–33; in California, 46–70, 93, 111; as celebrity, 83, 88, 121–22, 128–29, 130–32, 134; Codoman affair, 142–44, 156–57, 191–92; criticism of, 107–8, 127–28, 157–58; and Derby, 114–16; and doping horses, 34, 139; and Earl of Durham, 149–50; early races, 11, 53–55; in England, 96, 106–34, 136; false starts, 84–85; fines paid, 128; and forward-seat riding, 58–68, 83, 88–89, 93, 107–8, 115, 174, 191; fouls of, 142; in France, 112, 142–43; and Gardner, 143, 144, 156–57, 194–95; horses ridden by, 15, 84, 85, 87, 89; and inquiries, 144; Jockey Club discipline of, 153–56, 160–62, 176–77; and Keene, 97–98, 105; license refusal in England, 153–56, 160–62, 166, 176–77; in New York, 70–82; poem about, 122–23; politics affecting, 82; and Prince of Wales, 116–18, 131, 149, 151, 156, 160–61, 172, 191; and Smith, 89–90, 91–94, 119–20; and starting, 68–70, 84, 115, 124, 126, 128; as sulky driver, 93; suspensions of, 55–56, 140–41; training for, 10–11; winnings of, 55–57, 67–68, 84, 85, 87, 95, 109–12, 111, 112, 117, 126–27, 142

Sloan, Julia Sanderson, 169
Smith, Pittsburgh Phil, 40, 89–90, 90–95, 119–20, 170, 192
Spreckels, Adolph, 48
Stanford, Leland, 48

Starting: delays in, 45, 69–70, 84, 95, 147, 180; false starts, 69, 84–85, 115, 126; shootings over, 69; starting gate invention, 68–70, 84, 180. *See also* Horse racing
Stevens, John Cox, 98–99
*Story of a Bad Boy, The* (Aldrich), 3
Strychnine, 45
Sullivan, John L., 75, 88, 99
Surtees, R. S., 46

Talbot, A. L. "Professor," 6–9, 39, 133, 198
Tanforan race track, 48
Taral, Fred, 87–88, 128
Taylor, Smoky, 38–39
Ten Broeck, Richard, 104, 105, 106
*Tod Sloan by Himself* (Sloan), 2, 158, 160, 189–93
Trainers, 33–35, 37–39, 42, 138
Transcontinental railroad, 15
Trap shooting, 163–65
Travers, William, 17
Twain, Mark, 3–4, 48, 104, 193

Union Course race track, 15
Union Jockey Club, 47

Van Ness, Frank, 67

Vanderbilt, Consuelo, 129–30
Vanderbilt, Cornelius "Commodore," 29, 88
Vanderbilt, William Kissam, 129–30
Vaseline, 45
Victoria, Queen, 101, 161
Violence, 35, 39–40, 132–33

Warwick, Lady, 101
Washington Park, 20
Weil, Joe, 7
Western Union Telegraph Company, 178
Whitney, William C., 16, 78–79, 135, 145–47, 156, 162, 189, 193
Winkfield, James, 65
Wishard, Enoch, 138
Withers, 72
Withers, D. D., 16, 29
Women: as bookmakers, 23; at race tracks, 16, 18–19, 51; and Sloan, 88, 128–29, 158, 164, 165, 198
"Won't You Come and Play With Me?" 74
Wood, Charles, 176
Working class, 16

Ziegfeld, Florenz, 74, 77